THE SECOND MOUSE GOES DIGITAL

Self-Publishing Comes of Age

CAROLYN P. SCHRIBER

Copyright © 2017 by Carolyn P. Schriber

All rights reserved.

No part of this book may be reproduced in any form or by any electronic or mechanical means, including information storage and retrieval systems, without written permission from the author, except for the use of brief quotations in a book review.

ISBN-13: 978-0-9993060-0-0 (Kindle Edition)

ISBN-13: 978-0-9993060-1-7 (Print Edition)

Library of Congress Control Number: 2017916578

CONTENTS

About The Second Mouse Gets the Cheese	v
Prologue	1
1. Establishing Yourself in the Business	9
2. The Legalities and the Niceties	21
3. Building Your Platform	39
4. Choosing Your Software	61
5. The First Draft	79
6. Planning the Book	95
7. Doing Your Homework	115
8. Writing and Rewriting	137
9. Designing the Final Product	163
10. Choosing the Right Production Companies	185
11. Leading Up to Launch Day	203
12. Launching and Marketing	225
Epilogue	243

ABOUT THE SECOND MOUSE GETS THE CHEESE

Here's what reviewers had to say about the 2011 edition of this book:

"The Second Mouse had a lot to teach this old rat. It's a new game and a new field."

"Schriber's tone is humorous and her pace is lively, and I recommend her book heartily to anyone who is thinking of jumping into the world of the indie publisher. The Second Mouse gets an A+!"

"Any writer, even if they are hoping for traditional publishing, must read this book."

"Carolyn Schriber's easy writing style made me feel as if we were discussing these topics over coffee."

". . . invaluable information about how to dig your book out of the bowels of Amazon's bottom tiers to the light of day where it might get attention."

". . . an interesting and pleasurable read in its own right, thanks to the author's relaxed and friendly style."

"This book will serve as a reference for a long time to come and one I highly, highly recommend to writers everywhere."

"Carolyn Schriber, in a warmly conversational but still no-nonsense tone, provides practical advice and important warnings to anyone entering the area of self-publication."

PROLOGUE

So You Want To Write a Book

Hello. It's me—the Second Mouse. Remember me? I'm the one who got the cheese. As I contemplated the wisdom of issuing a second edition of my book on self-publishing, I started to imagine what I would say to budding new authors. The conversation went something like this.

My first question was, "How soon do you want to see your book in print?"

The writer shrugged. "Actually," she said, "I have all the time in the world."

"You're not in a hurry? Do you want to do it right? Then you have time to try the traditional publishing route. You'll start by trying to find an agent who is taking new clients. Then you'll wait for your agent to pitch the book to publishers. If she sells the manuscript to a publisher, you'll have to sort out the details of a contract. Then you'll spend weeks making all the changes the publisher demands. And then you'll have to wait until your book can fit into their publishing queue."

"That sounds like it could take years."

"Years? Probably so. And you'll be keeping your fingers crossed that an agent or publisher or editor does not go out of business, transfer to another company, or die."

"Does that happen?"

"Oh yes. When I was trying to find a publisher for *A Scratch with the Rebels*, my first editor took a better job with a different kind of publisher. The second found herself in a fight with the managing editor and had all her projects canceled. The third was forced by his university to take mandatory retirement before the book's contract had been signed."

"In that case, I think I've changed my mind. What if I say I want it done by next month?"

"You're kidding, right?"

"Yes, of course, but I would like to do it within the next couple of years."

"Good. Then you can devote the next year or so to learning what all goes into self-publishing. You can do this, but it will take both hard work and a fair amount of money."

"All right. Where do we start?"

"We start with another question. What is your goal for this book?"

"In my dreams? Fame and fortune. I want to hit the best-seller lists and do a coast-to-coast book tour."

"Really? Good luck! Here's what else you'll need. First, you must have a contract with a Big Five publisher. Why? Because when the *New York Times* compiles its bestseller lists, it only counts books sold by major publishers in major book stores. They don't care how many copies your grandmother buys. And second, major publishers don't send first-time authors on whirlwind book tours. Is your name James Patterson? J. K. Rowling? No? Then you'll need to tell your grandmother to save some of her book-buying money to pay your bus fare."

"All right. I'm daydreaming again. Maybe I'll just write a book about my family. I'll only need enough copies to pass out to everyone at my next family reunion."

"These are the people who knew you when you were ten—hair pulled back into pigtails, shiny braces on your teeth, coke-bottle lenses in thick pink plastic frames perched on your nose, and scabs on your knees, right? They loved you then. They'll love you now. Have fun with your project. Find a friendly local printer and make yourself a book. You don't need my help."

"No, I want to write a book that has a broader appeal than that. I'm not in this for the money, but I don't want to bankrupt myself, either. I want to self-publish a book that people will enjoy reading. And along the way, I hope to make enough money to pay the bills."

"Which bills would those be? You might pay your writing costs. But the mortgage? Not a chance. A new car? A trip around the world? Nope. You'll probably never make a living wage. I don't. But it is possible for self-published books to pay their way through the publishing process, with enough left over to finance an elegant dinner out or a quick research trip. You can do this if you are willing to do the hard work and if you have enough of a bankroll to finance the process before the royalties start coming in. We'll discuss how much you'll need in a few weeks."

It's Time to Take Stock

"I'm going to give you a list of qualities and characteristics you will need if you are going to succeed at this writing business. And yes, writing is a business, as you are about to find out. The first list won't be complete, but it will give you an idea of how well-prepared you are for the next steps. So go through these requirements and check off the items you can claim for yourself. Then we can start talking about them in more detail. And remember, it's not just important to know what you CAN do. You also need to understand what you CANNOT do."

- What kind of a writer are you? How's your grammar? Did you get an A in English class? When you read a book, do you see other writers' mistakes?
- What about spelling? Can you use a dictionary, or are you one of those people who can't look up a word because you don't know how to spell it?
- What about punctuation? Do you have a firm opinion about the Oxford comma? Do you even know what an Oxford comma is?
- How's your manual dexterity? Can you type? [I'm assuming you don't have a private secretary to do your dirty work.] Can you type WELL?
- What about other computer skills? Have you mastered Microsoft Word? Can you convert a document into a PDF file? Do you already have a favorite word-processing program?
- Is your computer new enough to run the latest programs? And does it have enough memory to store several versions of a 100,000-word document?
- Do you have access to a library? Do you have a library card? Have you ever used it?
- Do you have a place to write—a desk you can call your own, not a corner of the dining room table?

- Do you have the time to write? Can you look at your day-to-day schedule and identify some time that belongs to you alone?
- Do you write because you can't imagine a life without writing? Or does the idea of actually having to put words on paper scare you?

"The questions seem simple, but this is where we need to start."

"My answer to some of them is probably 'No.'"

"That's OK. You are identifying the areas you need to work on, not receiving a final rejection notice on your qualifications. Take some time to think about your weaknesses and what you might do to correct them. Then, if you're still around, we'll tackle some other requirements.

"Next, I want to know if you are internet-literate. Don't look that up. I created the word. Writers get to do that occasionally."

- Do you have a Facebook account? How many FB Friends do you have? Are they all family and school chums? Or have you thought about adding some writers and book publishers to your list of Friends? Many writers are open and eager to meet readers who are interested in their books. And it's easy to connect. Pick your favorite authors and search Facebook for their pages. Once there, ask to be added to their Friends list. Chances are they will agree, and you'll soon be picking up valuable writing tips from some of the world's best writers.
- Do you have a Twitter account? Again, check on your followers and look for new people to follow. Twitter makes it easy to search for writers, book lovers, publishers, and writing experts.
- Many people avoid LinkedIn, thinking it's just for business. Well, writing is a business. There are several

discussion groups for writers. Check them out until you find a companionable group of folks who are willing to share advice about writing and book publishing.
- Have you tried Pinterest? Creating and adding to boards about your favorite subjects is fun and addictive. Many writers use Pinterest profitably. I have a separate board for each of my books, and then those boards have spawned related topics—recipes from my stories, pictures of my characters, scenes from places in the books, and even guides for book clubs who might want to read the book.
- Have you tried Instagram? Internet audiences tend to be fickle, and at the moment, many of them are abandoning the older sites for the innovations over on Instagram.

"Is the internet all that important?"

"You bet it is! Especially for those who do not publish with one of the traditional Big Five publishers. If you are an indie author and publisher, your books appear in two formats—print-on-demand and electronic editions. Traditional book stores seldom carry either format, so where will your readers go to purchase your book? The internet, of course. Your readers are people who use their computers every day. They have Amazon accounts or Apple iBooks apps. If they look for your book in a Barnes & Noble storefront, they'll end up looking in an electronic catalog. Make no mistake. Without the internet, you won't be selling many books unless you spend your time going door to door or hosting wine and cheese parties.

"The formula is simple. You go where your readers are. And your readers are sitting in front of a computer or using a tablet or smart phone to find and order their reading material. Your readers are people who send emails or text messages, keep track of their friends' birthdays on Facebook, make snarky comments on Twitter, send out job applications on LinkedIn, put Instagram's rabbit ears on their friends' photos, and turn to Pinterest for ideas for tonight's dinner.

"Some of them—the most dedicated readers—will turn to Goodreads for guidance on what to read, check all the reviews of a new book on Ask David, and play silly matching games on Freado in hopes of snagging a free copy. They will google your name to find out who you are, and they will expect to find a website featuring your books."

"It all sounds overwhelming."

"There's no way to avoid our digital world. You need to start right now to build your internet presence. The big-name publishers may not have meant the internet when they demanded that an author have a platform, but it comes close. You must become active, friendly, and clever on the social media sites. You need to join Goodreads (which is now a part of Amazon) because your readers will expect to find you there. You need a great website—attractive, appealing, easy to find, easy to use, and full of interesting tidbits about yourself and your books. And finally, although possibly most important, you need a blog—one where you can talk directly to your readers, offering them the quality information they can only get from you.

"You won't become an overnight internet sensation. It takes a long time to break into this latest club, which is why it is vital that you start right away. My blog started with seventy-five readers a month. After the first year, that number increased to two hundred a month. The third year it jumped to a thousand, then ten thousand. Now in its sixth year, I often get 1500 readers a day. Do they all buy my books? Of course not. But lots of them do.

"If you have to choose between establishing your internet *persona* and writing your book, I suggest you hone your writing skills on internet posts. Save the book manuscript until you know readers out there are waiting for it. And then, you'll be prepared to write. The Digital Mouse stands ready to guide you on every step of the way. Let's get started."

ESTABLISHING YOURSELF IN THE BUSINESS
"Getting from There to Here"

It's the Second Mouse again. We met for the first time in 2011. I'm the one who first introduced you to the idea that you might be able to write that book you'd been imagining. Back then, I reminded you that while it is still true that the early bird catches the worm, there's not a whole lot to be said for that accomplishment—unless, of course, you're really into slimy things covered in dirt. I encouraged you to remember that it's the Second Mouse who gets the cheese, after the first one . . . Well, we don't need to go into that. I was just making a point: that you don't have to be at the top of a bestseller list to have a satisfying life as an author.

Why am I back, telling you the same things all over again? It's because the publishing world is changing fast. New ideas, new websites, new software, new resources, and new challenges face authors every day. You need to keep up with the latest innovations—websites, software, advertising schemes, and new publishers—if you want to hang onto your little wedge of the cheese. I'm still learning how to avoid the traps of self-publishing because the traps seem to multiply and grow more devious every day. I want to share what I'm learning.

Some of you, I'm sure, are thinking that a mouse probably doesn't know much about writing books, but you'd be wrong. Have you ever thought about how many talented mice fill the pages of our library collections and bookstore shelves? I'll be introducing you to some of them as we go along. I think you'll find they have quite a lot of mousey wisdom to share.

Let's start with my small contribution—the story of how I got started as a writer and how I decided that self-publishing was the right track for me. The story isn't new, and some of you have read parts of it before. But the message hasn't changed.

Less is More

For a while, my computer opened to a desktop picture that always made me smile. It showed two dandelions—one a full yellow bloom and the other a white seed ball, many of its seeds starting to fall and drift away. The caption read, "Less is more unless you're standing next to the one with more. Then less just looks pathetic." It's a rather gloomy perspective, I admit. The older seed head does look pathetic. Then I realized that it was the pathetic dandelion on the left that made me smile, not the one in full flower. That was when my perspective started to change.

Who can resist the white balls of down that appear when a dandelion goes to seed? We pick them, blow softly, and watch the seeds, each with its tiny parachute, float off to bloom again somewhere new. I tend to see this fully-developed seed ball as the young adult I once was. There was so much I wanted to do, and the parachutes pointed in all directions. I was a high school teacher, a wife, and a mother. Because of my husband's career, I was more specifically an Air Force officer's wife, with all the formal rules and expectations that went along with that identity. I could be a dutiful and unobtrusive helpmate, but I also had to be ready to step in and run the household when the Air Force shipped my husband off for a year-long remote assignment.

What all could I do with my life? I adopted stray kittens and nursed them into fat and furry adulthood. I loved to cook, so I took cake-decorating and gourmet cooking classes. I dug up sections of the yard to put in garden crops wherever I could find space, and I learned to smile when my three-year-old pulled up all my pumpkin seedlings to show me he knew how to weed the garden. I bought a sewing machine and learned to make my clothes. When a back injury sentenced me to a couch for long periods of time, I took up needlework. I read everything that had a printed word on it.

For a while, I was a church choir director, and more frequently I taught in whatever local high school had an opening. I had studied to become a Latin teacher, but the history of the people who spoke the language was also tempting. So I became a student again, picking up a master's degree in history just because I enjoyed it. Eventually, that path led me to more studies, a doctorate in medieval history, and a coveted tenure-track professorship. My dandelion puffball was still full of possibilities.

Eventually, of course, most of those individual seeds floated off somewhere. The husband retired from the Air Force, and then I no longer had to wear white gloves or attend Commander's Teas. There were spatial limits to kitten-raising (a maximum of four cats became our rule). The bathroom scales suggested that I curtail my cooking adventures. These days you're more likely to find me sautéing spinach than decorating a cake. Arthritic fingers limit sewing to the occasional button. Aging knees protest digging in a garden. A raspy voice problem curtails the singing. And even someone who has a cushy teaching job eventually reaches retirement age.

I've tried sailing off in many directions and watched other opportunities float away. Along the way, I've rejoiced, cried, experienced success, recovered from a failure, met stimulating people, and lost a child. And here I am, well into my seventies, feeling very lucky to have at least one little parachute left. I can still string words together, and I have a rich treasury of stories to tell. All the places I've been and all the people I've met enter into my books in some way. Now when I look at that dandelion picture, its perspective means something entirely different to me. It says I'm still here, standing straight up, writing furiously, and ready to make my mark.

A Writer's Identity

Many years ago, I retired from a career as a college history professor. I had a string of books and articles to my credit and some skills, like deciphering twelfth-century Latin handwriting, which was relatively useless in the real world. What surprised me was discovering that once I was free from the "publish-or-perish" rule of academia, I still wanted to publish. I knew I had always been a story-teller at heart. The stories behind the history were what fascinated me—not the dates or treaties or economic theories. But was I equipped to write fiction? That, I didn't know.

Making the switch from academic historian to historical fiction author required some fundamental changes in how I looked at writing. I had to re-think what was most remarkable about the story I was trying to tell. I no longer had to document my research or prove a point. Believe me, giving up footnotes after a lifetime of teaching careful documentation was painful. But then I remembered a prescription one of my advisers gave me in graduate school.

> "If your footnote contains information about your story, put it in the story," he said. "If it's simply a reference to your source, and if it's an indisputable fact, leave it out. Only footnote those ideas or details that are likely to antagonize some self-important old goat looking for a reason to be cantankerous."

Voila! My footnotes disappeared. And good riddance.

Other parts of my academic training, however, were impossible to jettison, and I think my writing is stronger because of them. First, I accept the fact that there are restraints on my imagination. I will never write a book about werewolves or space aliens, for example. I might enjoy reading such a tale, but my flights of fancy never stray beyond the possible. I can create a character and then imagine how that person will react in a given situation. I might even be able to write a story from a cat's point of view. But all my characters will resemble, in some form or other, people I have known or observed in real situations. I'm stuck with a focus on facts. Don't ask me to write a scene in which a six-eyed robot ends up in a fourth dimension. Even composing the preceding sentence strained my imagination. Fantasy? Can't do it.

Next, I believe firmly in doing one's homework, and I hold

writers to a strict standard of accountability. A historical novel must be historically accurate. Nothing irritates me more quickly than finding that an author has changed the facts to suit herself. There's a famous, award-winning movie, in which a newly-crowned king of England marries a French princess who immediately gives birth to the heir to the throne. He's a real king, she's a real French princess, and the child does indeed inherit the throne. But the movie sets the marriage some fifteen years too early, when the French princess was only three years old. If the story starts out with a horrible error, why should someone watch the rest of the film? Sorry!

When I started writing about America's Civil War, my desk always contained several types of resources. A multi-year calendar of the Civil War years allowed me to check every date and keep the chronology straight. A small pile of books offered details of clothing, furniture, tools, and recipes from the 1860s so that one of my characters did not sample a dish or use an invention before its creation. I even had a handbook of the native flora and fauna of South Carolina so that I could describe my scenery accurately. I didn't hesitate to "google" details to make sure my characters were believable. To keep the dialogue convincing, I had a dictionary of nineteenth-century vocabulary that I found indispensable. When one of my characters was a slave who spoke Gullah, both my editor and I tried to learn the basics of her language so her words would ring true.

To my delight, I've found that such facts do not usually bore readers. Small details may pass a reader's attention unnoticed, but the cumulative effect of factual knowledge is an increase in plausibility. These historically accurate details function to hold one's attention on a great story. In short, I have created my own identity as a writer of historical fiction—one who tells the stories behind the history.

Publishing Lessons Learned the Hard Way

One day I received the following query in my email. I'm not going to reveal the writer's name, although I do know who she is. She raised some important questions, ones that deserved a thoughtful answer.

> *I've been quietly following your blog for about a year now. Your topics are fascinating! I can get lost in historical research ... If I may ask, I'm quite curious to know why you chose self-publishing for your books rather than going the traditional publisher route? There are so many history buffs in the world, I would think there's a huge market for your work, both fiction and non-fiction, and you have the credentials to back you up. Was it to have more control over your work? Did you go through traditional publishers at first and they weren't interested? And, have you had success in self-publishing, volume-wise?*

I must start my answer by correcting a couple of her assumptions. There are many history buffs in the world, I agree, but that does not mean they make up a huge market for my particular book. I am constantly amazed at how narrowly some people limit their interests. I began by writing about a particular regiment—the 100th Pennsylvania Volunteers. One descendant of a soldier in that regiment sent me a note, saying he probably would not be buying my first Civil War book because most of my characters were in Company C and he was interested in Company K. Fair enough. He's entitled to his interests.

Next, my correspondent says I have the credentials to back me up. Again, not so fast. I am a trained historian—a retired Professor Emerita at a well-known liberal arts college. BUT ... My specialty as a professor was in the history of Anglo-Norman church-state relationships in the twelfth century. How's that for narrow? It means absolutely nothing to Civil War scholars, I can guarantee you.

The explanation of how I decided to self-publish is going to take some time, I'm afraid, because it was not a quick decision. It stretched out over a period of years. After I retired from active college teaching, I decided to follow up a long-repressed interest in America's Civil War because, for the first time, I was free to do so. Before retirement, I had published two books, but both observed the rules and standard practices of academic presses. I found publishers for both of them because (1) I was relatively well-known within the small subset of historians who were working on topics closely related to twelfth-century Europe, and (2) I was willing to accept the fact that I would never make a dime from those books.

Academic scholars write books to demonstrate that they belong in the profession. They write because it is necessary if they want to get a job, and it is an even bigger requirement if they want to earn promotion and tenure. The first publishing contract I signed guaranteed me fifteen cents per copy of my book—after the press sold the first ten thousand copies. Since there aren't that many people in the whole world interested in a monograph about the diplomatic maneuvers of Bishop Arnulf of Lisieux, I knew from the start that I'd never see that fifteen cents. I was content just to see the book in print and to know that other scholars viewed it favorably.

Now, let's jump ahead several years. It was 2003, and I was working on a Civil War history called *A Scratch with the Rebels*. It was based at least in part on some letters written by my great uncle. I had a good story to tell, the facts to flesh it out, and all that history training behind me. After I had written a few chapters, I applied for a National Endowment for the Humanities grant, hoping to finance my research trips to South Carolina. I didn't win the award, but one of the judges was sufficiently impressed with my proposal to mention it to a university press in the state where my regiment originated. The editor was quite taken by the idea, sent the chapters off to readers, and came back with a tentative offer. She advised me to make sure I was writing for a general audience and to concentrate on telling the story. While I waited for my contract to arrive, I finished the manuscript. Then my editor left for a better job without warning. The managing editor took over the project, put it on a back burner, and left it there for ten months. Then she informed me they were no longer interested.

Undaunted, I shipped it off to another university press where I had a contact, and at first, the new editor was enthusiastic. He sent it off to several prominent Civil War professors for comments. I should have known right then that I was doomed. Eventually, the readers' comments came back, and they complained that the approach of the book was not theoretical enough. One pointed out that I had failed to discuss all the relevant research that was going on in the field. Another said too much of the book relied on personal letters—a story, rather than historical records. My new editor tried, I think, to explain to my critics that I was writing a book for a general audience, not for an academic search committee, but in the end, it didn't matter. I had no reputation as a Civil War historian, and the field was simply not open to newcomers. That editor turned sixty-five, retired from his job, and the dog-eared manuscript came back to me—again.

It had been over three years by then, and I was discouraged. An email from the first editor urged me to give it one more try. She recommended a small private press that specialized in Pennsylvania history and the Civil War. Not bothering this time with a formal query letter, I called them. They asked for an emailed copy of the manuscript, and six days later, I had a contract in hand. Success? Not quite what I had imagined.

The people at the new press were open and friendly, and the royalties were three times what I would have received from a university press. There were drawbacks, however. I had no control over the layout or appearance of the book, which came out looking entirely too much like a junior high school textbook. Quality problems existed, too—the plastic surface on the cover began to peel almost immediately, and all the editor offered was a suggestion that I use a warm iron to reseal the coating before I tried to sell my copies. No one had ever warned me that a publisher would expect me to repair my books.

The company also turned out to be very inexperienced at marketing and distribution. The advertising fellow featured *A Scratch with the Rebels* in the catalog, but that publication only appeared a couple of times a year and went to people who had purchased other books from them. Their chosen distributing company failed to put the books out for display and simply returned the copies after a few months. In the end, the press sold only a few books, and my total royalties amounted to less than $25.00. The only books that did sell were those I bought myself at half-price and resold to my friends and at a couple of book signings.

By the beginning of 2009, I had devoted six years to *A Scratch with the Rebels*—with almost nothing to show for it. I had made some major mistakes along the way, I admit, but I also had learned that the publishing market for the average writer was a minefield. By then I was working on a new book—my historical novel, *Beyond All Price*. I knew I needed to find a new approach.

Becoming a Self-Publishing Author

Once I started working seriously on my Civil War novel, *Beyond All Price*, I also began looking for ways to publish it. Waiting until you have a finished product just does not work; you have to do your homework along the way. I started with the standard approaches. I found books written in my genre (in this case historical fiction set in the 1860s) and checked on their publishers and the authors' agents. These were names I could at least be sure would be open to the type of book I was writing. To that basic list, I added other publishing houses and literary agents I found listed in such resources as *Writer's Market*. I looked up each one on the internet to learn how they preferred to receive submissions. Each one on the list received a hand-tailored written or emailed query letter.

Responses were spotty. Almost half never replied. Some sent a canned message: "Sorry. We are not accepting new clients." Others said, "Sorry. We no longer welcome unsolicited manuscripts." Only a handful expressed any interest whatsoever, and they consistently asked for a full description of my platform before they would consider the book. At that stage, I had no idea what a platform looked like in the publishing world. I needed more information than the agents and publishers were providing.

Here's what I found. If you are a household word—a politician, a celebrity, a sports figure, or a best-selling author already—you have a built-in platform: a fan base of people who will buy your book because of who you are. If you're just a hard-working writer, you have to build a platform for yourself. Publishers and agents suggested that I needed the following:

- a dedicated website visited by hundreds of users every day.
- a blog that had a similar reader base and gathered dozens of comments on every posting.
- a personal Facebook page, with hundreds of followers and daily postings.
- another Facebook Fan Page, one focusing on my writing.
- a Twitter account, with frequent postings and thousands of fans.
- a LinkedIn account, with multiple recommendations and connections within my professional community.
- a personal mailing list of media outlets, bookstores, libraries, and civic organizations, all of whom would be eager to do interviews with me, invite me as a guest speaker, or host a book signing event.

Fortunately, I'm pretty adept at finding my way around a computer. I just had never bothered to become involved in social networking of this sort. I went to work, focusing on building my internet resources. These outlets are not hard to create, but they demand an enormous amount of time to develop their full potential. I have continued to work on this platform ever since, and my numbers after seven years of activity continue to grow. I have over 620 Facebook Friends, some 1200 Twitter followers, more than 740 connections on LinkedIn, and a website/blog that receives around 1000 hits a day. To me, that's amazing, but the figures are still not quite up to the five thousand guaranteed readers that most publishers want to see. At most, I have a good-sized soap box that serves as my platform.

One other factor weighed into my publishing quandary. The year 2011 marked the beginning of a five-year commemoration of the Civil War. Interest in Civil War history was at an all-time high, and I expected that enthusiasm to last for most of the next five years. But by 2016, we were all going to be tired of the topic. My window of opportunity was cracked, not wide open. If I wanted my new book to benefit from the increased coverage of the Civil War, it had to be ready to go. I simply did not have time to spend several more years pursuing followers, then agents, and then publishers. There seemed to be only one other path to putting the book into the hands of willing readers—self-publishing.

THE LEGALITIES AND THE NICETIES

"Everyone Needs a Neat Little Nest."

Did you ever read Beatrix Potter's *The Tale of Mrs. Tittlemouse*? In it, Mrs. Tittlemouse is a tidy little mouse who takes great pride in keeping her cozy house under the hedge neat, clean, and well-organized. She's never happier than when she is sweeping her floor or straightening the pictures on her wall. But several visitors disrupt her life. Bugs track in dirt, a spider leaves cobwebs behind, a slug leaves a slimy trail, and dozens of ants drop crumbs as they pass through. First, she fusses. Then she

pouts. And then she sets out to do all that cleaning and straightening again. She could teach new authors a lot about organizing their lives, their legal affairs, and their offices.

Formulating a Business Plan

It's one thing to decide you'll self-publish your new book. It's quite another to take all the steps necessary to become a publisher. Here's the point you must understand: publishing a book starts long before the book reaches the printed page. Publishing is a business, not an afterthought. So establishing a business was my first step.

Forming your own publishing company will make you feel important and make you rich! (Well, maybe not the rich part, but it is an ego boost.) More important, if you don't have a company imprint, your books will carry the name of the production company you use. That will leave an unfortunate impression, especially when most readers do not understand the difference between a print-on-demand company and a vanity press.

Starting your own business is as easy as just doing it. In many states, you don't even have to file papers until the business is making a profit of three thousand dollars. And in the meantime, while you are waiting for your book sales to make you rich, you can at least deduct your expenses from your income tax if you are the sole proprietor of a small business. What's not to love? Here's how to go about it.

A business needs a definition and a name. I started with the name, something I could use as a publishing imprint for my books. I didn't want anything that would identify me too closely—not my name or a street address, nothing too cutesy, but something that would lend itself to a neat little logo. After coming up with several ideas, only to discover by way of a Google search that others were already using the name, I looked around the room where I was sitting and realized that all four of my cats were there keeping me company. My first thought was, "This is like living in a cat house." Then, realizing the suggestive connotation of that phrase, I switched to German, coming up with Katzenhaus Books and a simple black cat silhouette as a logo.

Next, I asked myself what I wanted this business to do. The answer was straightforward. Katzenhaus Books would produce, publish, promote, and sell one or more works of original historical fiction. It would remain flexible enough to expand into other literary genres. Perhaps eventually it would be able to offer similar services or advice to other writers who were seeking alternative publishing choices.

Any business needs capital and a financial plan. During my academic career, I had relied on research grants to support the writing process, a publishing contract to pay production costs, and a publisher to bear the burdens of advertising and distribution. All I had to do was write. Now, all those expenses came back to me as a self-publisher. I started my financial analysis by comparing several years of our living expenses against our income to discover how much discretionary money I had available. After deciding how much I could afford to risk on this venture, I did some research on self-publishing companies to estimate the total cost of a typical book. What I discovered was a range of expenses, depending on how much help I was going to need.

The next step involved an honest examination of my knowledge and abilities. I had easy access to most of the research materials I would need, so I would not have to do a whole lot of travel. I'm a professional historian, a pretty good writer, and an experienced copy editor, I realized. The writing was not going to be a critical problem. Advertising and distribution remained question marks, but I had some background in doing book signings and conference presentations. I was also an experienced webmaster. When it came to book design, on the other hand, I was pretty much out of my element. While I might have an idea or two about how I wanted a particular book to look, I was going to need someone to do the actual cover and interior layout. It appeared that I could afford to pay for some contracted design services and handle production costs out of the nest egg I had identified. Then I worked on establishing a book price that would make it possible to recoup my expenditures.

My plan was to produce the book I was eager to write within the next two years. I needed to sell enough copies to (1) restore the savings account and (2) accumulate enough of a cushion to finance any future book. I gave myself an estimated eighteen months to two years to accomplish that. If at the end of four years, I had not made a profit, I would retire from the publishing business and take up knitting or crossword puzzles. I'll report on the outcome of that resolve when we get to the end of this book.

Tax Deductions for Writers

The Internal Revenue Service has a soft spot for writers. Who would have guessed! Once you admit that you are an author by claiming that designation as your profession, the tax laws are on your side. Someone in Washington understands that book production takes a long time, and that you can work at it for years without making any profit because you are still creating the book, not selling it. They will grant you your deductions for expenses for up to five years before they start refusing your claims to be a real writer. On your tax return, don't list yourself as store clerk or plumber's assistant while you are writing. There's a special designation for writers; find it and use it. The last time I checked, the Professional Activity Code for an independent writer was 711510. Oh, you definitely should keep your day job, but think of yourself as a writer and regard fry cook as your hobby, not the other way around. Then start collecting your deductions.

Next, take a look at the space where you do your writing. If you are using an old card table and a folding chair for a desk, you probably can't deduct what you paid for the furniture ten years ago, but if you go out and purchase a new computer desk, using it only for your writing, its price will be deductible. New or recent electronics (computer, printer, external backup drive) can be deducted or depreciated. The first phone line into your residence is not deductible, but if you add a second line for a fax machine or an 800 number for your business, you've found another deduction.

Be sure to keep track of all expenses for office supplies—pens, pencils, notepads, printer cartridges, thumb drives, scotch tape, paper clips, file folders, labels, a calendar, an appointment book, scissors, a rack to hold current file folders. Will you be mailing books to on-line purchasers? Those postage rates mount up fast. You can even deduct the cost of air if you buy it in compressed form and use it to clean your keyboard. (I use mine to chase the cat off the desk, but the principle is the same.)

Think about advertising. You can deduct anything you have imprinted with the name of your company or the name of your next book as an advertising expense. You'll need a supply of business cards, but you can also use the same size card to announce an upcoming book. (I had some printed with a picture of the Second Mouse on them. I have a second set of half-size business cards with photographs of Beaufort, South Carolina, on them to advertise my novel, *The Road to Frogmore*.) Both are deductible, as are bookmarks that match your book covers or brochures telling dealers and bookstores how they can order your books.

Much of your book budget will go for travel—to research libraries, book signings, or writing conferences. If you travel by air, your airline tickets are fully deductible. If you travel by car, you can deduct the exact mileage, provided you keep a log or record of the odometer. Your tax worksheet will ask for details of your car's purchase price, its year and model, its VIN, and its total mileage, so keep them handy. In 2016, the standard mileage deduction was fifty-four cents a mile if the travel was purely for business. I bought a magnetic company sign for under $10.00. On business trips, I slap that sign on the front door of the family sedan and turn the entire trip into a business expense. You can also deduct hotel bills, any parking fees, and road and bridge tolls if you keep records. You can even include one-half of all your individual meal costs. The theory there is that you'd always have to eat, but home-cooked meals are cheaper than restaurant fare.

And finally, you'll need to keep careful track of the books you order for resale. With a print-on-demand contract, you don't have to keep a huge inventory on hand, but you'll need a constant supply of printed books to give away, to send to book reviewers, to sell to your friends, to take with you to speaking engagements, or to enter into awards contests. You may be asked to report your sales and to pay a state sales tax, so you'll need to account for every copy you purchase. Be sure to check local municipal and state laws on sales tax. In my state, you don't have to report sales for tax purposes until your sales go over $3000.00, but that may not be so where you live. The books you sell will cost you a bit more than you anticipated when the tax bill comes in, but the books you give away become a form of advertising, so be generous.

For many authors, these expenses can mount up to a tax deduction of several thousand dollars. Just remember that the government expects a business to be earning a profit after five years of effort. If you have not made any money after five years, the IRS may tell you that writing is now just your hobby and deny any deductions. It will be time to declare your real occupation as a fry cook or plumber's helper. Even then, my accountant tells me, if you have a record of steady income from the sale of your books, the IRS will overlook the fact that your expenses are more than your profits. If you have cash coming in, you can still deduct any expenses that exceed your income.

The Home Office

Establishing a business office also has tax advantages. Once you have a plan and a named business, you can declare it as a sole proprietorship on your income tax and start taking deductions for all those expenses. The biggest deduction will come from establishing your home office as your principal, regular, and exclusive place of business. What does that mean? Well, no more writing at one end of the dining room table and then shoving the papers out of the way to serve dinner. You must have a defined space in which you conduct all the activities associated with your business—writing, researching, editing, advertising, shipping. It does not have to be a large space. You can fit an office into a walk-in closet, a cubbyhole under the stairs, in the basement or the attic, or into a different section of a room, separated from all other activities there. It simply must be used for your business and nothing else. You'll need a desk, a filing cabinet, and—most important—a place to keep everything separate from the other parts of your life.

Have you set up your home office? Then you have a place of business. Measure the space in square feet, determine the square footage of your entire house or apartment, and then figure out the percentage of the residence that you use exclusively for business. (A 10' x 12' office in a 1500 square foot house equals eight percent devoted to business use.) That percentage now applies to all of your housing expenses that affect the entire space—heating and lighting bills, rent or mortgage interest, insurance, homeowner association fees, a security system, and termite protection are all partially deductible expenses. You can't deduct painting the living room if you use the back bedroom as your office, but you can claim eight percent of the cost of a new roof since that applies to the entire structure.

I was fortunate to have my space already designated. When we moved into our new condo, we had the builders convert what started out as an open den area into a third bedroom with a small closet. My husband had already claimed the smallest room as his place to work on all his Lions Club business. This new room was to be mine. It has evolved into a cozy hideaway that makes a perfect home office. My initial requirements were these: a door that closes, lots of natural light, phone and computer cable connections, and a few creature comforts. I furnished it first with bookcases and a large slab table to serve as a computer desk. And here's what it holds at the moment. I've added risers at the back of the desk to lift frequently-used office supplies, the printer, the cable modem, the backup drive, and other components away from the main desk surface. Two short filing cabinets flank the desk to hold research files and other supplies while providing additional space to stack stuff. The closet is now full of industrial shelving to hold overflows of books, files, shipping supplies, and extra computer elements. An upholstered rocking chair and a floor lamp positioned between the accordion-fold doors of the closet provide a hidden reading nook. A futon, full of pillows and a fuzzy throw, waits for the moment when I need a quick nap.

The atmosphere is welcoming. The walls are a bright, energetic tangerine. A magnetic white board allows me to leave notes or pin up interesting pictures or publicity clippings. The large picture window looks out onto a grove of cedars and cypress trees. The rocking chair sits on an oriental rug, and a Tiffany lamp gently lights my desk area. On the walls are a few award plaques, my diplomas, and a huge etching of St. John's College, Oxford, where I was lucky enough to teach for three separate summers. And scattered around are a few stuffed animals from significant places—a bear dressed as a Union soldier from Gettysburg, another dressed as one of the palace guards from Buckingham Palace, the ragged little puppy from Poogan's Porch in Charleston, and the stately lion from the Biltmore estate.

Finally, there are the reminders of the purpose of this particular office. Above the entry door is a cutout of a black cat, looking exactly like the Katzenhaus cat from my business cards. A miniature brass Civil War cannon acts as a paperweight. The closet door sports a green street sign that says "Frogmore" in honor of one of my books. (And no, I didn't steal it; I bought it in a souvenir shop on St. Helena Island.)

The result is eclectic, but it is my principal, regular, and exclusive place of business. When I'm here, I'm working. Even the cats have learned to respect the boundary of the doorway. They will wander in once in a while, but only to curl up quietly on the floor or the futon, thus keeping it Katzenhaus in fact as well as spirit.

Assembling the Staff

Self-publishing is something of a misnomer. The process of taking a book from the first idea to a spot on someone's bookshelf is going to require the help and talents of many people. The heavy work used to be done by huge publishing houses. When you decide to self-publish, the responsibility for all the many tasks involved falls squarely on your shoulders. But you are already the author, the editor-in-chief, and the business owner. You cannot hope to sit isolated in your little home office and do everything yourself, no matter how talented you may be. The success of your book will depend upon how well you assemble a team of assistants. Here's a look at the staff I have put together. Perhaps it will give you some ideas.

My business plan recognized that I would need to hire a design artist to create my book covers and layout experts to make sure that the final books met the exacting requirements of the publishing world—standard page numbers, attractive fonts, spacing, chapter titles, and flourishes all in place. Since both those areas were way beyond my expertise, I hired both functions through the production company that contracted to produce the physical book. As it turned out, that was something of a mistake. Their work was adequate but not as pleasing to the eye as I had hoped. For later books, I hired separate designers for my covers and my page layouts.

I found another source of staff members at a company called Vistaprint. I got started there by ordering my first business cards for Katzanhaus Books. Through that one purchase, I learned about their other great promotional items and ended up buying a magnetic sign for the side of the car, postcards, brochures, a tote bag, and several other items with my logo on them. Then I found that they also provided hosting for websites and blogs, as well as domain names and email addresses for companies. I was able to use their services for all my early promotional and web-based needs.

Every writer needs a banker. Money is crucial to your success, but many people are not trained to handle it efficiently. I certainly wasn't. My first lesson came when a friend of a friend bought a book from me and handed me a check. When I looked at it the next day, I found that she had made it out to Katzenhaus Books. I took it to the bank, only to have it rejected. I couldn't cash it because I didn't have an account in the name of Katzenhaus Books. I could either hunt the person down and ask her to write another check (embarrassing!) or open a business account as Carolyn Schriber, DBA (doing business as) Katzenhaus Books. Since there was a real possibility that other checks would follow the same pattern, I went ahead and opened the account. It was a good move, as it turned out, since the bank provided an associated credit card that let me keep business purchases separated from household purchases. It also provided safe, direct deposits for royalty payments. That arrangement worked well until the bank decided to charge all company accounts a monthly fee that cut into my profits. I quickly changed banks to find one whose business accounts were free.

At about the same time, I realized that I needed to be able to take book orders on my website, which in turn meant I needed to have a way to accept credit cards. Despite what you may have heard, most people trust PayPal to manage their credit card purchases. The service they provide is the easiest—and the safest—way to handle such payments. I've never had a PayPal charge that bounced, and the company is quite good about forwarding customer information. They charge only a couple of percentage points on each transaction, and those are pennies well-spent for the convenience. Granted, occasionally I get a phishing attack on my account, asking that I send in my bank account number. But since all such requests are by definition fraudulent, there is no real danger of jeopardizing my private information. Further, PayPal is diligent about tracking down the perpetrators if you send them copies of any such emails. I use their services continuously without problems.

Recently I found another reason to work with PayPal. When you go out to do a book signing or to give a talk, you expect to sell some books to help offset the costs. And the chances are good that some of your customers will want to pay you with a credit card on the spot rather than with cash or a personal check. I had tried a couple of credit card services, including one that attached a small plastic square to my cell phone. But the process of handling those charges was cumbersome for me and, unfortunately, annoying to customers. Then PayPal came out with their credit card reader. It, too, plugs into an iPhone, but once I set it up, it became a simple matter to swipe a card, type in the charge, and let the customer sign by scrawling his name on my phone's screen with his index finger. Click one button if the customer wants a receipt, and the sales slip sails off to the email address associated with the credit card number. The deposit goes directly to my PayPal account. Simple. Safe. Secure.

To extend my outreach, I needed the help of professional promoters. I found assistance from three sources. First, the heavily-used reading site, BookBuzzr, created a free on-screen gadget for each of my books and continued to offer me new ways to advertise the books for free. I gained access to professional trade shows by subscribing to NABE, the North American Booksellers Exchange. The connections I have made through professional writers' organizations have also been invaluable. Writers are tremendously generous folks, probably because we've all been in the same trenches fighting the same wars. I've now added several more sites to my list of promoters—AskDavid, BookBub, and several others pass along tweets about new releases or special pricing deals.

When *Beyond All Price* began to make a lot of money—not a fortune, but more than I ever expected—I sought more help with money management. A financial advisor helped clarify the best uses for unexpected windfalls. He found flexible investment ideas that helped preserve the principle while providing a way to allow the income to make money on its own. He also introduced me to an absolute necessity—an accountant who could help me organize my records and deal with the tax complications that come with self-employment taxes and irregular income schedules.

Somewhere along the line, I received an email from an acquaintance who asked if I had protected the film rights to my books. At that point, I had no idea how to do it. But I quickly learned that I needed the advice of an intellectual property lawyer to guide me through the intricacies of formal copyright registration and to prepare a simple options contract that would guard against anyone snatching my story and profiting from turning it into a movie without my knowledge.

I relied on friends for many things. They served as sounding boards when I needed to talk through an idea. They volunteered as beta readers to check for unfortunate typos, blatant errors, and unintentional omissions. They were my first sales people as they talked about the book to their other friends, and throughout the process, they were faithful cheerleaders. A couple of them are still reposting my blogs and tweets to keep spreading the word. I couldn't have done it without them.

So there are the people I needed to self-publish a single book. Even I am surprised at how many there are: a design artist, a layout expert, a production company, a printer, a web host, a banker, a credit card manager, professional promoters, a financial advisor, an accountant, a lawyer, a sounding board, manuscript readers, salesmen, and cheerleaders. Each of them deserves partial credit for any success my book has achieved. If you're beginning this same process, start now to identify the staff that can help you along the way.

Creating Your Website

Once you have decided to open a website (an author page, a book page, or a company page), you'll have to make several important decisions. First, you need a domain name and a web host, somewhere to post your page. The possibilities are endless. Almost everyone has access to a server these days, and it can be confusing to know what will be the best deal in your area. Here are a few suggestions and some issues that might cause you trouble. First, claim your domain name by registering it with one of the several companies that handle these matters. Godaddy.com may be the best-known, but you can also use Register.com, NetworkSolutions.com, or WebsitePalace.com. They all provide the same services, so check carefully to see what each one charges.

You'll want to find a domain name that is short, simple, and relevant to the purpose of your page. Are you creating an author page? Then use your name. A book page? Use the title or an abbreviated form of it. A company page? Then you'll want the name of the business. (Avoid initials unless you're as well-known as IBM or AT&T). You may also want to register the same term with several different extensions so that no one can leap onto your fame and steal it for another site. So don't just register your website, SamSmith.com; you should also be sure to claim SamSmith.org, SamSmith.net, and SamSmith.biz.

Now you must choose a web host, and it is up to you to decide whether you want a free one or one that charges a monthly fee. Sound like a no-brainer? It's not. Free sites are widely available. Some of the best-known and most popular are on Google, or servers like Blogger.com or Yola.com. Your decision depends on the purpose of the site. For the last few years, I have used a free website on Blogger, where I could post some of the out-takes from books I was writing. The selections were there because I loved them, although they didn't fit into the current book. I offered them to my dedicated followers, who just wanted something new to read.

The site worked for a while because it suited my purpose, but it had several drawbacks. The assigned address of my blog was "ontheroadtofrogmore.blogspot.com." The inclusion of "blogspot" in the URL tells everyone that this is a free site, and savvy internet users—and most search engines—automatically reject it as not a serious site. I also did not have complete control of the content. I couldn't transfer the articles in batches, and Blogger could shut me down at any moment. I couldn't sell anything on the page or advertise my books, although pop-up ads not of my choosing might appear.

For my more serious website, the one that supports my independent publishing company and its publications, I use a paid site hosted by Vistaprint. Vistaprint also handles many of my printing needs, such as business cards, banners, brochures and items with my company logo, which means that my website can use the same graphics and match my other advertising items. I can use my own domain name—KatzenhausBooks.com—and use the pages, as I wish, to carry an order form for my books or to open it to other advertising. Although I have been generally well satisfied, the blogging feature is not working at the moment. I may have to move.

Other popular choices include Bluehost, Drupal, Wordpress, Dreamweaver, Powweb, Site Build it, or HostGator. Their options and learning curves vary significantly, so I recommend you survey them carefully before jumping to any one. Perhaps the best way to choose is to look at websites you like, and then consult with their owners to find out what host and software they are using. Take advantage of those who have gone before you. You don't have to reinvent the wheel to create a website. It can be as easy or as complicated as you wish.

Designing Your Webpage

I've been working on web pages since 1995, so I've seen a lot of new ideas come and go. Web pages are somewhat akin to fashion. What makes a page look bright and modern one day will stigmatize it as old-fashioned a week or so later. No one finds a plain white page with small black type attractive, but add one too many colors or pictures and you have a site people will hate because it's too busy. So where is the line between dull and gaudy, between childish and hopelessly complicated? Here are a few tips I've picked up along the way.

Your page must reflect the subject matter it contains. You can't sell cheese on a flower-strewn background, and it takes a talented florist to work a skunk into an ad for roses. (Actually, I've seen that one, but the florist's name was "Pugh.") When I was running ORB, the Online Source Book for Medieval History, my page designer came up with a lovely medieval scene for our headline banner. The first edition of *The Second Mouse Gets the Cheese* shows a cartoon mouse throughout the chapter headings, so the title of the book page used a cartoon font. There's considerable room for error, however. Littering the page with too many mice will eventually irritate your viewers. I recommend picking one element to show the theme and then letting the page's information carry the theme from then on.

Flash introductions used to be popular, as did animated gifs, which had little characters running across the computer screen. They are no longer surprising. Now they just delay the appearance of the real information, and impatient readers will move on. The same caution applies to sound clips. I considered using a cheer on the web page for the online book launch I ran one year. Then a reviewer complained. She tried to visit the website at night while other family members were asleep. She was not amused to open the page and be greeted by a raucous crowd. Neither was her sleeping husband.

Other types of animations cause serious problems for viewers with physical limitations. Flashing lights, waving flags, or other sudden or rhythmic visuals may trigger seizures or migraines in those who are susceptible to such stimuli. Those who are color blind will miss parts of your page if the contrast between print and background is not great enough. Keystrokes that require two hands may be impossible for some. Information conveyed only by sight will be lost to those who are blind. Illustrations always need to be labeled with tags for those who use software such as Jaws to read what appears on the screen.

The quickest way to learn how to design your web page is by visiting the pages of others. See what appeals to you and what doesn't. Note that too much information is a turn-off. Pay attention to the ease with which you can navigate the site. Are the buttons or links marked and in a logical spot, or did you have to hunt for them? Was vital information available quickly, or did you get lost trying to find what you needed? Design your page to make it easy to use.

For a book or author page, the most important elements should appear at the start—a cover shot and a professional photo of the author (not a snapshot of you at your senior prom). Contact information should also come early. Today's readers want to know the person behind the book. They want to be able to follow you on Twitter, to connect on Facebook or LinkedIn, to send you an email. I don't recommend ever giving out your home address or phone number; I use a post office box for the address of my publishing company. But it's vital to let your readers feel that you are a real person, one with whom they can communicate.

What else do your potential customers want to find?

- They want to know a bit about your book—why you wrote it, who your characters are, where and when it takes place, what crisis or problem the main character faces. Tempt them by telling them just enough to spark interest; don't give away the ending.

- They want to feel important. I try to include a few out-takes from my writing—extra descriptions the page readers will see. I also use photographs. When I first put up the pages for *Beyond All Price*, I included head shots of the real military figures in the story, as well as some 1860s pictures of the locations in which the story took place. While I was still working on *The Road to Frogmore*, I posted some then-and-now shots of Beaufort, SC, and St. Helena Island. Only faithful blog-readers got to see them before they ended up on one of my Pinterest boards.
- If you plan to do book-signings or public speaking engagements or radio interviews, be sure to post your schedule. You might increase your audience. Even if your readers can't attend these events, they'll feel connected to your activities.
- Customers also take vicarious pleasure from any awards you receive, so be sure to brag a little when one comes your way. Post a picture of your medal or the fancy sticker on your book.
- Has your book received a favorable review? Post a copy so that potential readers are tempted to buy the book.
- Consider including a formal press release, just in case the visitor to your site is a newspaper editor, or the alumni director of your old school, or your local librarian. We'll talk more about press releases in a later chapter.
- Finally, make it easy for the web visitor to order your book. Set up a PayPal account and take orders right from your website. Or provide working links to your book's sales page on Amazon or another retail source.

Your website should make every visitor feel welcome, and it should offer enough variety to invite a second visit. Think of it as your place of business, and let it reflect the very best of you.

That's the take-away from this chapter. If you secretly regard your writing as a hobby and relegate it to those moments when you have nothing better to do, you are doomed from the start. If you really want to be an author, you must treat writing like a business. Set up your office, take care of the legal matters, get your finances in order, think of readers as customers, and get to work.

BUILDING YOUR PLATFORM

"Finding the Important Things in Life"

Do you remember the story of Stuart Little? If you are an early Baby Boomer, you may have read the book by E. B. White, which came out in 1945. If you were born closer to the end of the twentieth century, you probably watched a movie with the same title—a live-action and computer-generated film from 1999. In both, the main character is a charming and lovable little mouse who is a part of a human family. In the book, Stuart was born as the second child of the Littles, a human couple with a human first child named George. In 1945 children were not expected to question where babies (mouse or human) came from; by 1999 the story changed to Stuart's adoption from an orphanage. In either case, Stuart struggled for acceptance. His brother George refused to admit he had a mouse for a brother, and the family cat, Snowbell, resented a mouse who was a more beloved member of the household than the pet cat. The book and movie plots differ considerably, but both involve a series of accidents that could only happen to an anthropomorphic mouse. Stuart gets rolled up in a window shade, dumped into the washing machine, and carted off by a garbage truck.

So what does Stuart Little have to teach us about publishing a book? Well, throughout his troubles, Stuart remains open to making new friends—a bird, a neighborhood cat, or a group of schoolchildren who are bored by their arithmetic problems. In every case, Stuart reminds us that everyone is important and that it is wrong to judge people by their size or appearance. If Stuart popped up in your writing nook today, he'd probably scare you. But then he would tell you that using social media is a great way—although not the only way—to make new friends and to spread the word about your writing.

Mount Your Platform

You are standing under a virtual spotlight, notes in hand, ready to talk about your book. Who is your audience? Where's your platform? Your platform consists of all the contacts you can make with people who might be interested in buying your book and reading your content. The internet has made it possible to reach out to audiences all over the world. Now you just need to start establishing your presence and meeting your potential fans. But how do you know which of your followers will be interested in your book? You can waste a lot of time pitching to people who simply aren't interested.

Many Social Media sites have millions of users, and they come in all sizes, shapes, and attitudes. Some who visit your pages will be more interested in your wallet than in what you are writing. It's wise to be selective about which followers to accept. Here's an example that happened to me recently. I received an announcement about a new subscriber on Twitter. The username was "The Love of Sex," and the description announced that this person has four followers. Yes, that's right—four! Does anything about that sound suspicious to you?

All right. Maybe this subscriber is a brand new user. But if you were opening a Twitter account to appeal to those who love sex, would you choose as one of your very first followers an old retired and widowed professor who lives with four cats?

If The Love of Sex wants to read about my books, I can't forbid it, but I'm not going to reciprocate and follow him back. I doubt we have anything in common. I'm willing to bet this was a variation on an old phishing technique, and that a day or so from now, The Love of Sex will no longer appear on my list of followers because he was not really looking for a good historical novel to fill his lonely hours. Not everyone who follows you is looking for what you have to offer.

Facebook

There are dozens of social media sites on the internet, and I am certainly no expert on all of them. The big three—the ones most often used—are Facebook, LinkedIn, and Twitter. They serve different purposes, and I've been surprised to see how different their audiences are. I'll try to show you how I use each one to promote my work, and you can apply the same lessons to another site if you like.

Let's start with Facebook, which now, as of Fall 2017, has 1.32 billion active users who log on daily. You probably count a few of those subscribers among your personal friends and relatives. I have no intention of telling you how to use Facebook. As I write, the powers behind the scenes are still re-organizing and tweaking what materials you can see, and what others can learn about you. If you're going to use Facebook, that's the first thing you'll have to accept. The website changes. Sometimes it changes several times a day.

On my own Facebook account, I have now accepted over 600 friends. They include a few family members; a neighbor or two (although that strikes me as silly); some long-lost high-school classmates; several former students, some dating back over twenty years; and a large contingent of academics—mostly medievalists or colleagues with whom I worked at Rhodes College. The rest are members of Lions Clubs International, both locally and around the world. What can they possibly have in common? I know them. I'd recognize them on the street. I'd probably hug most of them. They are all people with whom I have shared both common interests and common experiences. We've worked together, struggled with the same problems, and shared our ideals and goals. I care about them and how they are doing, and I hope they care about me.

When it comes to posting my status on Facebook, I try not to bore anyone, or irritate them unduly with efforts to sell my latest book. But if I've had an exciting day—or a miserable one—these are the people with whom I can share it. I post pictures here, both of myself so they can watch me age and of my current activities. So it is on Facebook that I am most honest about my thoughts and opinions. What good does that do for business, you may wonder? Many of my Facebook friends will buy my books; others will be tickled for me when I win an award. I benefit when they talk about me or leave a congratulatory note on my wall. Facebook friends can form a virtual cheering section in your life.

There's another side to Facebook, too, one that is still evolving too rapidly to lay down strict guidelines here. Anyone with a personal Facebook account ought also to be aware that it is possible to build extra Facebook pages that advertise your business, or your favorite non-profit, or your club. On those pages, you can reach beyond your circle of friends to tap into those mysterious 1.32 billion users who are reportedly out there. If you're new at the game, develop your page first, and then think about expanding to these fan pages.

LinkedIn

My second social media outlet is Linked In. This site is much more business-like than Facebook. I have 741 connections on Linked-In, and almost none of them are cross-overs to my list of Facebook friends. I know less than half of them personally. My LinkedIn connections are the power-brokers in my world. There are a few former students, but they are not the ones who just want to reminisce about college life. These are graduate students, or lawyers, or business people who are making a difference in their world. They've sought connections to bolster their resumes, and they realize that a former professor is a prime candidate. Many of my connections are members of Lions Clubs International, but they are not local members. They are the leaders in that organization—former international officers, staff members, or CEOs of Lions-associated non-profit organizations. They are people I can turn to when I need business advice. The rest are business figures with whom I have had some dealings, as well as media and public relations people.

How can they help build my publishing platform? Well, my financial advisor, my lawyer, and my accountant are on that list, along with public figures who can orchestrate newspaper or television coverage when I have an announcement of a new book or an award. They are the people who can help set up book signings or public speaking engagements. They are great resources because they have extensive contacts. I try not to bury them beneath my sales pitches, and I don't overtly try to sell them anything, but I can trust them to help me make my name better known.

Name recognition is a vital advantage offered by LinkedIn. LinkedIn also lets people with shared interests create discussion groups, where they can connect with those who have similar interests or who are facing similar problems. I currently participate in several writers' groups, as well as one that discusses fund-raising ideas for non-profits.

Twitter

And then there is Twitter. What can you possibly accomplish with 140 spaces? (This is not a political question!) The easy answer, of course, is that it teaches you to cram a lot of information into the smallest possible space. Brevity is good. But beyond that, I see Twitter as a conduit—the vital link between me and the vast world of the internet. At the moment I have around 1200 followers on Twitter, and I'll be the first to admit that I don't know many of them personally. We are strangers who have made a brief connection because of a third party who knows us both, or people with whom we share a mutual interest. They are people who might care about what I have to say. When they follow me, anything I post will automatically appear on each of their Twitter feeds. They may—or may not—see it. But when they do, they each have the option of passing it to their followers, giving my message access to untold numbers of readers. Twitter can also send automated messages for me and share my posts on my other social media outlets.

Here's how it can work. Suppose I've just finished a blog post announcing the publication of a new book and including a link to the book's order page. I send it to my 1200 followers, and Twitter also posts it on my Facebook page (+600 readers) and my LinkedIn profile (+700 business leaders). Then a fellow writer in England retweets it to her whole list (+1000 fans). The president of a writers' society to which I belong retweets it to her list (+1250 authors). And three faithful blog followers in Missouri, California, and Colorado send it to all their friends (+1700 total). That one personal message reaches nearly 6500 people within minutes. That's the best, and easiest, advertising I know.

Pinterest

I have an on again, off again relationship with Pinterest. A while back, I decided to take down all my Pinterest boards because of my concerns about copyright issues. I was bothered by a requirement to list the source of each pin, which often turned out to be impossible. I was reluctant to accept the idea that I was giving Pinterest exclusive rights over everything I pinned. I was nervous about being sued by someone who suspected that I had infringed on copyright, no matter how unintentionally. And it seemed to me that Pinterest was encouraging people to ignore copyright laws; as a writer, I had to oppose that.

On the other side of the argument, came these facts. Pinterest seems to be relaxing their source requirements. The little URL box has disappeared. Pinterest is growing at phenomenal speed, catching up with the other social media sites. And it addresses the very demographic that I want to attract to my books. So, somewhat hesitantly and reluctantly, I am dipping a toe back into these copyright-threatening waters.

I'm starting out with a promise to myself—limiting my pins to photographs I have taken myself, or to those that come from websites like the Library of Congress, which states that use of their illustrations does not require permission. For many people, such limits would be impossible to sustain, but for someone who wants to pin about the Civil War, it's easy. The pictures that tell my stories are usually 150 years old.

I have to admit that there is something very addictive about those boards. I've already posted over twenty of them. Some are designated to illustrate the books in my series, The Civil War in South Carolina's Low Country. Two others—one dealing with 19th-century medicine and the other with 19th-century foods—are based on two little e-books that I published and eventually took out of circulation.

Others are touristy—my photographs of St. Helena Island and Fort Donelson, or cities like Charleston and Beaufort. Another section deals with the rest of my life by showing some of my community-service oriented activities, and, I confess, a board dedicated to the cats of Katzenhaus Books. Most recently, I've been adding guides that book clubs can use with each of my novels. They contain pictures of people and locations, recipes for foods in the book, additional reading lists, and possible discussion questions.

My hope for this new effort is two-fold. First, I realize that a period of history some 150 years old is unfamiliar ground for most readers, and I want to share as much knowledge about what life was like as I can. I hope that pictures of the people, the places, and the events that occur in my books will make the stories come alive. And second, I want my readers to feel that they know at least a little about me. I enjoy those moments when I can get out and talk to a group of readers, answering their questions and sharing my enthusiasm for the Civil War. But since those opportunities are limited, this business of pinning boards offers another way we can communicate between reader and writer.

Instagram and YouTube

According to the bean counters who study such things, many younger internet users are migrating from the big three (or four) I have listed above to spend their time with visual images on Instagram and YouTube. That's not surprising, given what we know about the time children now spend looking at screens rather than the world around them. It's not good news for writers who still rely on words to convey their stories, their beliefs, and their fantasies. Perhaps we can lure these children away from their back-lit screens to delve into the pages of a book, but we may need to use visual imagery to do so.

The Second Mouse, however, freely admits to knowing almost nothing about these latest social media sites, so for the moment, we will skip over them. A word of caution about the usual social media sites may be necessary here, however. Readers turn to Twitter for pithy sayings, not to be told, "Go buy my book." Facebook provides enough ads as it is. Don't make it worse by using your status updates as just another ad. Your readers are probably interested in your signings, your awards, your public speeches—but don't beat them over the head with demands for their money. YouTube videos can reach huge audiences, but don't post something unless it makes you look like a professional, not a silly amateur turned loose for the first time with a cell phone. An Instagram headshot of an author sporting rabbit ears will not do much to convince a reader to open her book. And LinkedIn audiences are even tougher. The participants there are usually serious business people. Give them the information they can use, not blatant self-promotion.

Some General Rules about Social Media

As a former teacher, I always expected a standard reaction when someone asked me what I did. I got one of those recently. A woman was doing her best to connect with me at a stand-up cocktail party. She was new in town, managing a small office that provides business services to harassed executives. She finally quit talking about her company and asked me what I did. I told her I was a writer, and she looked puzzled. "What do you write?" she asked. "Historical novels," I replied. The look on her face said it all. She might as well have just stepped in a nasty sidewalk doggy mess. "Oh," she said, and then she was gone—abruptly, without a word of transition. She had just marked me as an untouchable. OK. I guess she wasn't much of a reader. But I'm hoping she was also an exception.

One of the most surprising things I have had to learn since I started writing was that most readers like writers. Real readers get excited when they find out that I'm an author. They want to learn about my books. They want to know how I do what I do. They want to talk about characters as if they are our mutual friends. But there's still a problem. I don't want to be the obnoxious character who walks into a room saying, "Here I am—an author—please come do me homage." And making those connections is even harder in social media situations. So how do you turn a stranger into an adoring fan, or at least into someone who knows your name? Here are a few tips I picked up at a recent writers' conference.

- Be friendly and give yourself time before you make a judgment call. Show that stranger that you are truly interested in her, no matter how odd she is. After all, she might give you the seed from which to grow a new character.
- Be willing to work with others who love and write books. Share your readers with other authors and help

publicize their books. Mutual interests make good friends.

- Keep your troubles and traumas out of your internet posts, or at least use two accounts, one for personal life, another for the business of writing. Whatever you do, don't whine!
- But do share the fun things that happen to you—not how much money you just made, but the strange red chicken that wandered into your yard. Talk about the activities that give you pleasure, the kind deed you observed someone else do, or a particularly lovely moment. Let readers see your personality.
- Encourage your readers to express their opinions on a controversial issue, but avoid taking a stance that will alienate some of them. I wouldn't endorse a political figure, for example, but I would speak out about the need to have a public vote on an issue that is causing concern. Here, we recently had a controversy over whether wine sales belong in grocery stores. Getting the question on the ballot was a tough fight, so I was comfortable urging people to sign that petition without telling them which side I would support.
- On Twitter, try using a robot to schedule your postings. That will let you make sure you are not saying the same old thing to the same few people over and over again. Bookbuzzr.com is good for this because you can see a list of your posts, and schedule them so that they do not repeat at the same time or on the same day.
- If you're trying to encourage people to buy your book, use your blog or Facebook post to talk about the writing process, the problems you have had with the story, or the research you have done to make the setting come alive. Sell yourself, not your book.

Getting Started as a Blogger

The internet also offers a chance to talk directly to your readers by publishing a blog. The best way I know to start a blog is to start. My first efforts were sincerely uninteresting, but I kept at it until I received some comments that let me know what my readers were thinking. In my case, they wanted to know how and why I chose self-publishing after writing several books with established publishers. Once I addressed some of the lessons I learned along the way, readership blossomed. When I first started my blog, I was getting about sixty hits a month. Now I get between 25,000 and 30,000 a month. I just checked the figures on this week's blog and discovered that I set a record of two million all-time hits.

I found that one effective way of gaining readers is to do a guest blog for people who are already fairly well established on the blogging scene. When I started, I offered my services to several writers whose work I enjoyed reading. Most were delighted to allow me to appear as a guest on their blog. Their readers who saw my article clicked on the links I provided to my blog and came back if they liked what they read. That's one reason why my numbers have soared.

What other advice can I offer? Stick with it. It takes a good six to eight months before you gain a foothold in the blogging world. Consistency with regular postings on same days of the week helps. Whenever possible, add photos relevant to your topics. Remember that statement about younger readers gravitating to Instagram? Pictures attract attention. Having an interesting site helps, too. But you can produce great content, have a creative blog design, and write regularly—all without attracting a single reader. The real key to starting a blog and keeping it going lies in your ability to connect with your potential audience. You will need a network of social interactions. Think of your blog, not as a monologue or a lecture, but as one side of a conversation, and keep links going between your blog posts and what's happening on your social media pages. Read other blogs to find great writers who are talking about the things in which you are interested. Follow the ones you enjoy reading. Comment on their content as frequently as possible. And when someone tries to open a conversation with you, respond to comments and emails quickly. Readers will come back to your blog again and again if they feel they know you as a person.

Making Money from Your Blog

There are many different approaches to writing your blog. It all depends upon your goals and the topics you choose. I'm going to skip lightly over the question about monetizing a blog because I've never attempted that. I know that a few people blog directly to make money and are successful at it. I read a couple of them. A local woman started blogging about her baby's life and has been entertaining readers for years. We've followed her struggles with depression, her move to bring in some money by advertising baby items on her blog, her leap into big money and the challenges that caused in her marriage. We suffered with her through the birth of a second child with developmental problems, her divorce, her experiments with becoming a vegan and a long-distance runner. She's brutally honest (and sometimes quite vulgar) about her feelings, and that keeps her readers coming back.

Another blogger wrote about her rescued kitten, and since nothing succeeds on the internet quite like cat photos, she rapidly became a spokesperson for all cat-lovers. She doesn't hesitate to pull on her readers' heartstrings. One year her cats even sent their own Christmas card to every follower of the blog. I admit I was thrilled to get a card from Waffles.

Those bloggers, however, already had a huge blogging audience before they started carrying ads and making money. Your valuable material comes first. Getting readers comes next. Once thousands of people read you every day, you might be able to get rich. Until then, however, I would put that goal aside and concentrate on building an entertaining blog. Be patient and write interesting articles. Distribute them. When your blog is running smoothly, you can think about compiling an anthology, selling it for smart phone applications, and you'll be on your way to a much better income than pennies for advertising.

If, however, you are determined to try to turn your blog into a cash cow, there are several things you need to understand. First, almost all bloggers who expect to make money from a blog will fail. They fail because they are amateurs at marketing and half-hearted in their efforts to monetize their sites. You can't just put up one little ad in a corner somewhere and hope readers will click on it often enough to generate a cash flow. You will have to choose the products you advertise with care so that they appeal to your readers. Don't try to sell sporting goods on a writing blog; try pens or computer software instead. Be sure that what you advertise is reputable and of high quality. If your reader buys a pen that doesn't write from your site, you will receive the brunt of the anger by losing a reader.

Be sure you have thought through your business plan, particularly if you are planning to sell your books through your blog. You can't sell items until you have figured out the details of how you intend to accept payments (PayPal may be the safest and easiest method), shipping methods and costs, and the tax laws of your state. You may need to incorporate your business and file regular quarterly tax reports.

You can't run your blog as a business if you are computer-illiterate. You will have to be able to use blog publishing software and social-networking sites. You must understand such things as HTML coding, RSS syndication, SEO (search engine optimization) tagging, pings, and trackbacks. And if those terms mean nothing to you at this point, you're just not ready to monetize your blog.

Even the host of your blog is important. If you choose a sponsored blog, you need to know how much control the host will give you over your postings. Don't try to sell items on a blog if you do not own the URL of that blog. One acceptable host choice is WordPress, although it has a rather steep learning curve. Have a young grandchild handy to explain things if you decide to go that route. I used to avoid Blogger because of URL issues, but they have since changed their policies and made the site much more appealing. I currently use a paid hosting service that lets me sell items through PayPal, but I cannot use ads provided by Google's AdSense. The arrangement suits me, but it may not suit you.

All of those warnings bring us back to the original point. For most people blogging is NOT a way to make money. It is, however, an excellent way to get your name out there. Many publishing companies now insist that their authors have blogs because a great blog provides a potential reading audience for the next book you write. In the long-term, your blog may result in increasing your income, but it will probably be a catalyst, not a direct revenue source.

Finding a Support Group

Recently, I had a message from a company that wanted $500 to enter my book into five different book contests. I didn't take them up on it, although I agree with the basic premise—that winning a book award, if the group is a prestigious one, is almost sure to result in an upturn in book sales. But $500 worth? I doubt it. I would much rather see a new writer use that $500 to attend a conference of writers. It doesn't have to be a fancy meeting. Sometimes the smallest ones are the most useful. A conference has one huge benefit over the book award contest—everybody wins. You get to spend two or three days in the company of people who think as you do—who understand the agonies as well as the delights of writing.

No one will bombard you with the kind of comments we've all learned to hate. You know the ones—the folks who say:

> "Gee, books are so expensive. You writers must all be really rich."
>
> "My Aunt Gertrude wrote a book once. Would you like to read it?"
>
> "Can you get me a publishing contract, so my book will get made into an HBO movie?"
>
> "It must be nice not to have anything else to do all day but just sit and write."
>
> "I just finished reading your book. Hurry up and write the next one."

Best of all, you will be meeting people who have faced the same sort of problems you face. And they'll be willing to offer you valuable advice. Writers may not be wealthy, but they tend to be generous with their time and knowledge and experience. A writers' conference is the place to tap into what they have to offer.

One example of this occurs every September in Colorado. The Rocky Mountain Fiction Writers meet for their Colorado Gold conference to encourage each other, to learn new techniques, and to recognize the best of their efforts. I've never had the privilege of attending a Colorado Gold Conference, but as a long-ago resident of Colorado, I still lurk on their web pages and read about their successes. I was interested to note, a couple of years ago, a new turn of phrase that appealed to me. One of the Colorado attendees commented that attending their meeting always felt like going home, like re-discovering family. She coined the term "my herd" to describe how her membership in the group felt. For a western-based group, of course, the term "herd" is particularly appropriate, and I fully understand what she means when she says, "I have found my herd."

And that got me thinking. Every fall, I attend the annual

meeting of the Military Writers Society of America. We have a membership of well over one thousand now, all of us with some connection to the military. We write about the military, or we served in one of the armed forces, or we married a serviceman, or we grew up in a military family. We have the same sort of bond that the Colorado writers define as being part of the "herd," but that term won't do for us.

We're not a herd, but what are we? A force? That sounds too much like Star Wars. My Marine brother would have suggested corps. My husband would have preferred flight. But we also have Navy members—a crew?—and Army veterans—a squad? It occurred to me that we are a regiment in numbers, but that sounds too regimented!

Unless somebody can come up with a better term, I'm going to think of the MWSA meeting as getting to see my troops. These troops are my people. They are generous, welcoming, and encouraging. They will send me home with a new resolve to write better, to write more, and to believe in myself. I need them, and I need that yearly transfusion of energy.

My advice for any writer is to step away from the keyboard for a few days. Take the time to find your herd, your troops, the people who let you feel like one of the family. And then absorb all they have to offer you. I promise it will make you a better writer.

Get the Most out of a Writers' Conference

As a former academic, I thought I knew what my first writers' conference would have to offer, but I was completely wrong. I was used to meetings like the American Historical Association. Everyone was there to find a job, to get a book published, to meet the editor of a journal who might be interested in their dissertation topics, to discover what schools were going to be hiring in the next couple of years, or to impress the academic community with their accomplishments. Those conferences were cut-throat affairs. Hiring committees watched job seekers with critical and disparaging eyes, looking for flaws or lapses in behavior or judgment. Job candidates checked out their competition. Everyone dressed formally to look as grown up and successful as possible. The pressure was intense.

Then I attended my first Military Writers Conference. People dressed casually, more interested in comfort than in style. Old members greeted newcomers with a hug, not a handshake. Casual conversation groups formed, scattered, and re-formed as attendees circulated. People seemed to like one another. Meals were pick-up affairs—pizza, tacos, make-your-own sandwiches. The bar opened early, and discussions ran late. Laughter reigned. I was amazed! This conference was a different world, and I had much to learn about how to find my way in it. So here are some tips I picked up.

Be prepared to make friends. Writers tend to be introverts. We work alone most of the time, huddled over a keyboard or prowling through dusty library archives, but we love discovering other people who think and work as we do. It surprised me to learn that rivalry and competition hardly existed among fellow writers. Instead, I found an atmosphere of camaraderie, an eagerness to share, and a willingness to rejoice in the small victories of others. So put on a smile and introduce yourself. You'll be an insider in no time.

Another trick I learned—if you want to meet people, volunteer to work a shift at the registration table. You'll get to see the entire list of attendees, so that names start looking familiar. Even better, you'll be the first person new members meet. If you're open and friendly, they'll remember you.

Don't expect everyone there to be a writer. If you listen carefully, you'll also discover editors, agents, small publishers, cover designers, readers, illustrators, graphic artists, legal experts, publicists, reviewers, and interviewers. These are the people you will need at some point in your writing career. Here's your chance to start making the right contacts.

Don't venture into a conference without a pocket full of your business cards, and be sure to collect full contact information from those people you meet. Once you get home, it won't do you much good to remember that guy named Jim or John or somebody who did file conversions. Try to get email addresses, too. You'll want to keep the conversations going and the contacts connecting. Be sure to send personal thank-you notes to anyone who was helpful or interested in your work.

Handle self-promotion gingerly. There's a fine line between letting people know what you do and coming across as a pushy jerk. Don't wave your book around. Some conferences let you bring several copies for sale. They may even have a display table and someone to handle sales for you during the meetings. Or they may have rules against selling. Don't guess. Find out in advance. The same kind of rule goes for other promotional materials. A conference is not the place for sell sheets and rack cards, although free bookmarks are sometimes acceptable.

Attend every seminar or lecture you can, and take notes. Start with the assumption that everyone in the room knows as much or more than you do about the process of writing. So absorb as much as you can. Ask questions, but don't turn a question into a chance to deliver your mini-lecture on the topic.

While you're there, you should also try to gather the details about the other services the organization offers its members. MWSA, for example, publishes a quarterly print and electronic magazine with payment for short articles, occasional small-group writing workshops, and an annual book contest.

Above all, get to know the other writers. They will be, far and away, your best resource. The friendships you form at a conference carry over for years. Other writers are the people you can turn to with a plot dilemma, to be a sounding board to try out new titles or cover designs, to tell you gently when you are heading in the wrong direction. Other writers make great beta readers who can catch those silly mistakes that your proof-reading may have missed. They can be called upon to write early reviews, to provide the perfect quip for your cover, or to recommend your book to others. They may also turn out to be some of your closest friends.

Some Writers' Conferences to Consider

I have not included specific dates or website URLs because these vary from one year to the next. However, you can find any one of these organizations—and many others like them—through a simple search engine.

In the Spring:

- San Francisco Writers Conference in February, for both self-publishing and traditional presses.
- SleuthFest in Boca Raton, FL in February. Mystery, suspense, and thrillers.
- South by Southwest (SXSW) in Austin, TX in March. Music, comedy, film, IT, and blogging.
- Northern Colorado Writers Conference in Fort Collins in the Spring. All genres and skill levels.

During the Summer:

- Historical Novel Society, alternating years between North America and England in June.
- Philadelphia Writers Conference (PWC), held in the Historic District of Philadelphia, in June.
- Writers' League of Texas, Austin, TX in June/July featuring editors and agents.
- Midwest Writers Workshop, Muncie, Indiana, in July. Meet industry experts and successful writers.

- Sewanee (TN) Writers' Conference in July. For poets, novelists and playwrights with manuscripts ready for critiquing.
- Romance Writers of America Annual Conference, somewhere in the USA in July.
- Women and the Civil War, somewhere east of the Mississippi in July. The roles of women (North or South) during the war.
- Thrillerfest in New York City in July. Educational program and big-name authors.
- Texas Association of Authors, Houston TX, in July, offering a marketing certificate.
- Writer's Digest Conference in New York City in August. Pitch your book to the publishing industry.
- Killer Nashville (TN) in August. Mystery authors and screenwriters.

In the Fall:

- Historical Writers of America in New Mexico in September.
- Military Writers Society of America, somewhere in the USA in late fall. Writers who have military backgrounds or military subject matter.
- Lost Lake Writers' Retreat, in Lincoln, Michigan, in October. Lessons, journaling, and writing time.
- James River Writers Conference in Richmond, VA, in October.
- Women Writing the West, rotating through western states in October. A place to meet editors and agents.
- BookBaby Independent Authors Conference, Philadelphia in November.
- Rocky Mountain Fiction Writers, Colorado in September.

Other More Frequent Meetings:

- San Luis Obispo NightWriters, monthly round tables and critique groups, annual Golden Quill writing contest, central California.
- Story Circle Network, headquartered in Austin, TX, but activities take place in local Story Circles around the country. Helping women tell their stories.

Many people will tell you that writing is a solitary and lonely affair. To some extent that is true. You may need to shut out the world before you can enter the world of your own imagination. Putting words on paper involves applying one single seat of pants to a solitary seat of chair. But never forget that those words are meant to reach others. Writing may, in fact, be the most effective and long-lasting means of communication between individuals. Your social interactions will open the door to becoming an author.

CHOOSING YOUR SOFTWARE

"Poverty with security is better than plenty in the midst of fear and uncertainty."

Does that quote sound like something from Aesop's Fables? Maybe that's because it is the moral of Aesop's story about the Town Mouse and the Country Mouse. The Town Mouse came to visit his country cousin one day, and the Country Mouse scurried to feed him well on wheat stalks, acorns, and roots, with a drink of cold, clear water. The Town Mouse turned up his twitchy nose and ate very little, but he told his cousin all about the fine foods and luxuries that were available to him in the town. The Country Mouse decided to visit and see for himself. The Town Mouse led the way to an abandoned banquet table, still full of fine cheeses, sweetmeats, jellies, and pastries. They had just settled into the feast when in came the house cat, followed by the servants and the house dog. The mice fled in terror. The Country Mouse had learned his lesson. "We each have to choose for ourselves," he realized, "and as for me, I prefer security rather than uncertainty."

Is there a message there for would-be writers as well? Of course. Software choices exist by the hundreds, some of them carrying hefty price tags, and each one promising to do more than all the others. So how do you choose which ones will serve you best? Which ones will keep all your information secure, even if they leave your bank account a little smaller? No one can answer that but you, Country Mouse. All I can do is tell you about the ones I trust with my files, book manuscripts, and permanent records.

Microsoft Word

Let's start with one universal and unavoidable fact: you must use Microsoft Word. No, I haven't become a shill for Microsoft Office, but I've learned the hard way that I must use it. My original word processing preference was Word Perfect, and back in the day, I even taught classes on how to use it. But, RIP, WP died a natural death, overcome by market forces that passed it by with features Word Perfect couldn't duplicate.

I learned to use Microsoft Office products at work when my college made a bargain deal and replaced all of our computers with ones that ran Windows and other Microsoft programs. I didn't think that it was an improvement. I found many of the features annoying. In my professional life, I needed a little jargon and a lot of Latin terms. Word's automatic spelling correction regularly changed what I was trying to write. I spend a lot of time muttering, "Curse you, Bill Gates," at an uncaring computer.

My next attempt to avoid what I saw as a threatening behemoth involved finding other word processing programs designed for Apple products. Open Office seemed like a safe bet for work I did at home. I installed it on my little laptop but soon discovered it had all of the drawbacks of Word without many of the benefits. Next, I tried Pages, but it, too, proved cumbersome. It produced documents that I could transfer to Word, but that didn't solve the problems; it just postponed them for a while.

Once I started to self-publish my work, I had to bow to the inevitable. Was I ready to send my manuscript off to a programmer who would do the coding for electronic editions? He wanted the file in .doc or .docx. Was I ready to publish the manuscript on Kindle? The instructions directed me to enter a .doc file. Did I plan to convert the book to various electronic formats by using Smashwords' Meatgrinder? Send them a .doc file. Did I want a layout designer to format my book for a trade paper edition? Start with a .doc file. That requirement has become the industry standard. It's an argument we independent thinkers can't win.

The bright side, however, is that it is possible to make life somewhat easier by doing your preliminary draft in your chosen word processor. You don't have to switch it to Word until you are nearing the finish line. And then you will discover one advantage to Microsoft's domination of the field. Word is so powerful that it can gobble up almost any competing format and transform it into a workable .doc or .docx file. True, switching processors in mid-manuscript may be an extra step, but it may save you months of grumbling frustration.

An Ode to Scrivener

I prefer to use Scrivener as my software for novel writing. Those of you who have participated in NaNoWriMo may already be familiar with it because Scrivener helps sponsor that annual orgy of writing bliss. Now that it is available for both MAC and Windows, I can't imagine anyone needing anything else. It's an endlessly versatile program that manages to keep almost every item of the book-writing process in one spot.

There's a section for research, which can hold notes, pictures, maps, and "messages-to-self." I keep lots of pictures there so that when I am writing about a particular location or character, I can open a picture and see it on my screen while I write. That adds detail to my descriptions and saves me from making silly mistakes about things like what is visible from a front porch or whether a character sports a mustache. In fact, it has a whole section for character sketches. I can fill out the questions about each of my characters, defining their back story, their foibles, their nervous quirks, their speech impediments, their hair and eye color, their family relationships—whatever is important to define the character. Then while I am writing, it is easy to click on a character name in the left-hand column and jump to a description.

Scrivener provides a separate template for locations, too, where I can record thing like trees, flowering bushes, wildlife, smells, and sounds. Is the land overgrown with vegetation? I need to list what kinds of plants grow there. Are bugs relevant to the story, as they may be for mine? Then I can add their characteristics here. My location files have pictures, of course, but also descriptions of the smell of pluff mud and the clicking sound palmetto bugs make as they stomp across a wood floor.

These are the materials I find helpful when I'm writing, but they may not suit your style at all. Part of the genius of Scrivener is that it lets you design your preferred work surface. You create the information blocks you need. Then you place them wherever you want them. You eliminate unnecessary distractions and make the changes you want to see.

How do you like to work? Do you write in chapters or scenes? Scrivener offers you both options, and once you have all the parts in place, it can put the entire manuscript together for you—in the right order, with chapter numbers. Are you used to working with index cards? Scrivener can show you your material in that format, with little cards tacked to a virtual cork board. You can color-code the cards, and you can move them about, just as you would if you were tacking them to a wall. I just used this feature to outline all my chapters.

Worried about formatting? Don't be. Is it a novel, a poem, a screenplay, a scientific treatise? Name it, and Scrivener formats it. Write with whatever fonts and colors suit your fancy. Then when you have finished, just tell Scrivener how you want the manuscript to look. Does your agent or publisher want to see it in double-spaced Courier? No problem. Are you going to self-publish? It can handle that, too.

Do you want access to an earlier version of your manuscript? You can import the whole thing, and then quickly move sections from the old to the new version. Want unique sections to store your materials? I've set up a section for ideological clashes that plague my characters, and another for specific quotes from my characters' journals and letters.

Do you prefer to see all your materials in front of you, spread across the screen? Scrivener has a three column layout, with your writing space in the middle, a listing of all your files on the left, in what they call a Binder, and an editing column on the right, which you can fill with whatever you need. Want more or less writing space? Stretch it out or shrink it. Want a blank screen with nothing but your words filling the screen in front of you? You can do that, too.

So this is the program I set up each time I start a new book. By the time I fill out my sketches and chapter headings, my planning stage is more than complete. Along the way, I decide who's NOT going to be in the book. I kill off all the unimportant folks and dump their first draft chapters and character sketches into a holding tank labeled "Outtakes." They're easily retrievable if I change my mind. Once I'm sure they are dead, I'll move them to the Trash where they will linger until I decide to empty the whole file.

I find the Scrivener format a help from the first moment when I start to plan my book. I identify my main character and some secondary ones who will play important roles. I outline all the ideological clashes and the main themes. I complete a plot outline, with the important points highlighted. Now all I have left to do is write.

Scapple

A few years after Scrivener gained popularity, the same programmers came up with a new piece of software to make writers' lives even easier. The title Scapple has no literal meaning. It's not a scalpel, which is a surgeon's knife, although Scapple often seems to me to be used in the same way. It helps me cut through the details of a story to get to the heart of the matter. The word also sometimes reminds me of a scaffold and can be used in the same way to provide a skeleton or support for a new book.

In its simplest form, Scapple is a mind-mapping application. It opens with a blank screen. Each time you type a phrase or idea, the words appear in a moveable box. Each box can hold a single word or a whole paragraph. The borders expand to provide whatever space you need. With a screen full of such boxes, you can begin to drag items around and connect them with various lines or arrows to show their relationships. You can use it to show the organizational structure of a company. You can build a family tree to show several generations descending from a single couple. I use it that way when I write a novel so that I can keep all the brothers and sisters, aunts and uncles, cousins, and spouses straight. By adding birth and death dates to each boxed name, I avoid making chronological errors. And for novelists, this is a great tool for illustrating the story arc, so that the writer knows what events are connected and in what order they occur.

But the real selling point of this new program is the way it can integrate seamlessly with Scrivener. Here's how I used it to write this book. I started by creating a box for each chapter in the first edition of *The Second Mouse*. Then I started moving the topics around, adding some, removing some, and combining others, until I was satisfied with an outline of twelve new chapters. For each of those chapters, I created connected boxes for the topics within the chapter. The "Platform" chapter, for example, started with a breakdown into "Social Media," "Websites," and "Writers' Organizations." And each of those could be broken down even further. Social Media had connected boxes for Facebook, Twitter, LinkedIn, and others.

Then came the real magic! On the left side of my computer screen, I displayed the Scapple outline of topics. On the right side of my screen, I opened a Scrivener document for the new book. The left-hand column of that display showed a binder containing little except for a title page, a copyright page, an empty table of contents, and a trash file. I set the middle (or content) section of the display to "Group Mode" and then selected "Cork Board."

Next, I highlighted parts of the Scapple diagram and dragged them—along with their lines and arrows showing relationships— right out of Scapple, across the computer screen, and into Scrivener's middle column. Without further help from me, those individual boxed notes became index cards on the cork board, arranged into stacks, which could be opened to show the contents of each stack. And from there, the major topics appeared in the Binder as folders containing individual document files. With almost no effort, except perhaps the suspension of my disbelief, my new Scrivener Project had a complete Binder index, ready to be filled and expanded.

Dropbox or iCloud?

Has one of these scenarios ever happened to you?

- You're in an airport, facing a long delay between flights, and you realize you are going to miss a deadline. The document you need to submit within hours is on your home computer, and you have nothing with you but your smartphone or a laptop. You need Dropbox.
- Maybe you've just finished deleting a bunch of outdated files, only to discover that you also deleted something important. You need Dropbox.
- You're on vacation and want to send some great photos to a friend without revealing your location to all of Facebook. You need Dropbox.
- Or maybe you're in a library with dozens of shelves of books on your research topic, but you can't find your working bibliography. You need Dropbox.

When I was working on my doctorate, back when computers were a rarity rather than a fact of everyday life, one of my professors advised keeping a copy of our dissertations in a fireproof spot. She suggested the oven since most ovens are well-insulated. Her second choice was the freezer. "What will you do if there's a fire in your building?" she asked. "Years of work could be turned into ashes in minutes." That was enough to give any graduate student nightmares. I didn't try the oven trick. I was afraid someone in the family would turn on the oven to preheat it without looking inside. But I did keep a copy of my dissertation in the freezer!

Today, of course, the recurring fear is more likely to be a computer crash—one unprotected by a backup file. Gremlins attack files without warning. The power goes off before you save. Someone accidentally empties the Trash. If you've never lost something you were working on, you are either incredibly lucky or more careful than anyone I know.

I'm sleeping better these days because I now use a simple but elegant program called Dropbox. This form of cloud computing saves and protects anything I store in it. It makes my saved documents instantly available on any computer or mobile device I may use anywhere in the world. And, if I make changes to one of those documents, it syncs the changes on all my devices, so that the newest version is always awaiting me, wherever I may be. This magical little blue box icon sits on my top toolbar, right next to my volume control and my date/time stamps. It's that critical to how I manage my files.

Dropbox offers one terabyte (that's 1024 gigabytes) of storage for $9.99 a month or $99.00 a year. The program works on almost any computer or mobile device. I have it on my desktop, my iPhone, my iPad, and my laptop, but I've also been able to use it on the computer in a hotel business center by entering the URL that links to my Dropbox. You can open your Dropbox without being online, too. If you deposit a new document, it will sync with your other devices as soon as you go back online.

This storage system provides other services as well. For a writer, it provides an easy way to send a preliminary manuscript out to beta readers. Rather than e-mailing each of the volunteer readers a separate file, you can do a group e-mail, giving them a temporary URL that will allow them to download your new book without accessing anything else in the Dropbox. You can share photos or music with your friends by providing them with a link to the files in your Dropbox. And best of all, it has a thirty-day backup feature for any file it contains, even if you delete the original on your other devices.

For me, this is not a question of Dropbox or iCloud. I use both, but for different purposes. I keep iCloud running on my computer in case of a sudden disaster. I appreciate knowing that my files are backed up somewhere. But for my writing files, I still use Dropbox. In it I keep a master file folder for each of my books. And into that folder I place everything—drafts, research files, pictures, timelines, genealogical charts—whatever resources I've needed for that book. When a question arises, I can go back and find that elusive detail that might otherwise disappear into a cloud.

I have to admit that Apple's iCloud, at the rate of $0.99 per month, is cheaper to use. So why don't I just use iCloud since I'm a MAC user? Dropbox's easy file transferring is one good reason. I also find Dropbox more logical in the way it organizes its documents. I prefer being able to see exactly where all my materials are. Somehow—and maybe it's because I don't fully understand the newer program—iCloud feels a bit mystical. It promises that all my files are safe in its fluffy floating storage heaven, but I have to take that on faith until I summon the one I need. I prefer the visual reassurance of Dropbox to the blind faith of iCloud, even if the cost of Dropbox is high.

Evernote

Six years ago, the third application in the trinity of software I used was a program called Evernote. By rights, it should have been called every-note, because that's what it will hold. Like Dropbox, and to a lesser extent, Scrivener, Evernote uses cloud computing to make sure you are connected to your work, no matter where you are. You can install this program on Windows or MAC desktops, almost any smartphone, laptops and note-books, and tablets such as iPad. Every few minutes, Evernote syncs your files with all your electronic devices. You can start to write an article at your home desk, add notes from your iPhone during a bus trip, stop in the library to add some bibliographic entries, and finish the final draft at your desk at work. Traveling? No problem. Just log onto your account from any computer, and edit that article. At least that is the promised scenario.

The Evernote design starts with a single note. You give it a title, a tag or two, and start typing. You can attach photos, audio or video clips, data files, websites, and PDFs to that note if you like. Once you have more than one note, you have the beginnings of a note-book, which can hold as many notes as you like. And if you have several related note-books, you can arrange them in a stack, which will only count as one of your permitted 250 note-books.

Let me give you an example of how I used this application. I had a stack related to each book I wrote. So, imagine a stack called "The Road to Frogmore." In that stack were several note-books. One was labeled "Characters." Its notes contained character sketches of each character in the book. There were also note-books for "Plot Points," "Settings," "Historical Events," "Photos," "Maps," and "Bibliography." There were similar stacks called "Beyond All Price," "A Scratch with the Rebels," "The Second Mouse Gets the Cheese," and a mysterious one provisionally called "Gus." And each one contained several note-books.

But not all my note-books were related to writing. I also had one on "Trips," one for "Recipes," one for "Media Contacts," and one for "Christmas." All the notes were searchable by their tags, even across stacks, so that I could turn up a 1860s Christmas dinner menu in one note-book and find a recipe for Christmas fruit cake in another. And then I could use those details in a book chapter about Christmas with the Roundheads.

Evernote also prides itself on building a whole community for its users. They have a blog where users can discuss new ideas and an ongoing library of instructional videos. They also feature what is called the Evernote Trunk of compatible products and services. As just one example, *Crafts Magazine* provides whole note-books of recipes and Do-It-Yourself projects that you can download for free.

There are, however, lurking problems. If you already have a note-taking program that works for you, you probably will not want to take the time to re-type all your materials. But for anyone who is just starting to get organized, I recommend this application highly.

Or at least I did at one time. That was before my notes began to overflow my computer. Having sufficient memory became an issue, since there was almost no way to remove a note-book or a stack once I had formed it. I began to feel like one of those little old ladies who keep every newspaper and ad that arrives in the mail—until every room is stacked floor to ceiling with useless paper.

I haven't used Evernote in several years, and I don't miss it. The truth about note-taking, for me at least, is that I store masses of notes in folders while I am working on a book, but once the manuscript is complete, many of my notes prove themselves useless. Out they go, as easily as dragging the folders to the trash. These days I try to simplify my life rather than filling it with trivia.

TimeLine 3D

Almost all stories will involve the passage of time, whether the action takes place within a few days or over the course of several years. Authors can easily become confused by dates, leading to a novel that becomes impossible to follow. The problem becomes particularly severe for the writer of historical fiction since many readers will already know about many of the events and will be quick to spot a discrepancy in dates between fact and fiction.

Here's how I approach the challenge. I use a timeline creator program for MAC called, appropriately, Timeline 3D. It allows all sorts of variations and creative designs. For each event, you can add a title, a date, a photo, and an explanatory sentence or two. I start with a basic file showing the most significant events of the Civil

War—battles, major troop movements, elections, and acts of Congress. Then I add the details of my fictional characters' lives—birth and death dates, schooling, marriage, entry into military service, and other events that are relevant to the story itself.

Finally, I create an "Export" version of each file and then paste the resulting texts into a standard Excel worksheet, one after the other. Running a "Sort A-Z" operation combines the lists and rearranges all the entries into one chronological file. After that, I can sort out the important events from the unimportant details and begin to see a basic outline of the book-to-be. This step also allows me to catch any unfortunate errors in chronology.

There are, of course, many other ways to approach this problem, and lots of other software companies to provide the tools. What matters is that you take the time to discover what happened, and in what order. Then it becomes easy to identify the arc of your story—the dominant goal, the crisis points, and the resolutions. Time(lines) well spent!

Grammarly

My newest software is an electronic editor. Several applications like this exist, and Microsoft Word even comes with a pretty good spelling and grammar checker. Grammarly, however, is my hands-down choice for ease of use, thoroughness, and helpful explanations. A free version is available, although it is pretty much limited to the same spelling and grammar errors that Microsoft catches. The free version is sufficient for a teenager trying to impress her English teacher, but it's not precise enough for a professional writer. The paid version, however, catches some 250 kinds of errors, many of which even the eagle eye of an old English teacher and a paid editor did not spot.

Here's how it works. The author imports a file into the Grammarly application. Currently, the program is not robust enough to handle a whole book manuscript at once, a deficiency the company promises to keep working to correct. For my current manuscript, I broke the content down into several files averaging around 20,000 words and fed them through one at a time. When I finished correcting all of the errors, I exported the separate files into their .docx formats and then copied and pasted them back together.

It takes only a couple of minutes for the Grammarly application to open your file, which now appears with every critical error underlined in red and a red-lettered explanation in the right-hand margin. Wherever possible, it will give you a suggestion, this time printed in green, of the necessary correction. If you accept one of their recommendations, you click on it, and it magically appears within the text. No more danger of making another typo when you try to correct an error. The application will usually give you an explanation of the original problem, so you'll be learning along the way. A caret (^) at the far right of the suggested correction will open further information. A small x will allow you to ignore the recommendation, although if it's a critical error, the program may come back to the same mistake several times before giving up the argument.

The premium edition also offers all kinds of corrections of diction. These errors show up in yellow to indicate they are less vital, although no less important. It will call your attention to such offenses as vague words, overused words, passive voice, frequently confused words, or general wordiness. And again, you'll be learning as you go along. It won't let you use the same word over and over in a single paragraph. The program won't let you say that someone walked without suggesting more vivid verbs—strolled, hopped, sprinted, limped, shuffled. It also comes with a built-in user dictionary, so if you happen to need many unfamiliar or foreign terms, it will mark the word the first time as "not in dictionary" and then give you the chance to add the word, so that it doesn't keep appearing as a mistake. That's a handy device for novelists whose characters may have unusual names.

Be prepared to be shocked at your ignorance. My recent manuscript of 83,000 words came back with 1738 errors. I was indignant at first. I'm an old English teacher after all! But what an improvement I saw when I reread the corrected manuscript. The text flowed more smoothly than my original version. The conversations were more natural, the descriptions livelier, and characters more personable. This program is a keeper. It's not perfect. I'm currently fighting an ongoing battle with it over the use of "gender-specific" words. My new book takes place in the 1830s, and one of the characters is a woman who inherits a business and finds herself struggling for acceptance from the men with whom she has to negotiate. Grammarly objects to the use of the term businessmen and wants me to substitute some phrase that is not limited to one gender. But of course, the whole point is that she is a woman in a businessman's world. Perhaps that is an argument that an algorithm cannot handle.

Other Grammar and Spell Checkers

In the course of preparing this chapter, I examined several other applications that offered similar editing services, but none of them came close to Grammarly. One called GrammarCheck looked promising. It promises to catch plagiarism as well as errors in grammar, punctuation, spelling, word choice, style, and sentence structure. The cost, however, is prohibitive. At $29.95 per month, it is not a program an author can keep using over time.

Hemingway Editor is much cheaper, with a one-time charge of $19.95 to install the app on a desktop. This one skips the usual spelling and punctuation checks, leaving those to the automatic functions of a word processor. Instead, Hemingway focuses on readability. It marks sentences that are too long or wordy in yellow. A red highlight means the language is too dense or complicated. Single words in purple advise using a shorter equivalent—"use" instead of "utilize" for example. Blue highlights adverbs and other weak phrases, and green marks passive voice. It's an interesting approach, but the application so far is limited to examining short passages, like a blog post or a newsletter. It cannot handle even a short chapter, which makes it unhandy for most book authors.

Scribens was the only free application I examined. Like Hemingway, it uses colors to highlight errors and comes with separate downloads for various browsers and packages like Microsoft Office. It checks for frequently-used words and other stylistic problems, along with the usual spelling, grammar, and punctuation errors. Scribens' analysis, however, seemed shaky. It classified every long sentence as a "run-on" sentence, disregarding the usual definition of that term. And when I found a spelling error ("ponctuation") on its website, I decided that free might be too high a price.

The bottom line on all these smaller editing applications is that while they can be helpful when an author's eyes are too tired to spot common errors, none of them is as good as a human editor. Language, it would seem, is more complicated and nuanced than most mathematical formulas can handle.

Vellum

Even while I worked on the final draft of this manuscript, I was getting ready to test another piece of software that promises to revolutionize the way authors handle their layouts and manage other design features. Vellum automates the layout and design process for both e-books and print editions. The price looks steep at $199.00 for e-books and $249.00 to do both e-books and print. It's a one-time charge, however, capable of being used for as many books as you like and inexpensive compared to the cost of hiring professional layout designers and electronic formatting experts.

As the previews and tutorials promise, the process is quick and easy. And so it is, up to a point. As with any such software, the more you ask it to do, the more complicated the task becomes. An early iteration of a digital formatting job seemed to do a credible job. There were, however, problems with spacing, headings, and chapter breakdowns. We'll discuss the specific changes that I needed to make when we get to Chapter 10 on designing the final copies. For now, let's just note that Vellum will do whatever you tell it to do, but you have to be sure you are speaking its language.

As a general rule, I found that the less formatting I did as I was writing, the easier the final transformations became. Take, for example, an embedded document like a personal letter. The first time I put it into the manuscript, I sweated over the challenges of indenting both margins of the quoted material. I could indent the left margins with a single key stroke, but it was nearly impossible to make the same change for the right margins in Scrivener. With Vellum, I could have left the quoted material unchanged. Then when formatting the Vellum input, I blocked the whole letter, and the program automatically indented both sides. The same rule applies to other elements like bulleted lists.

In brief, formatting with Vellum is a three-step process.

First, you produce a .doc or .docx file of the entire manuscript, making sure that there are no spelling errors or typos and eliminating as much formatting—things like double or triple spaces between paragraphs—as possible.

Then you import that entire file into Vellum and proofread it again, looking for errors that may have been introduced by coding variations. And this stage is where you will add special formatting details like block quotes or numbered lists. You'll be able to tell the second version from the first because the imported version's icon will have the Vellum flower on it.

And then you generate the formats you want, taking the time to specify any particular coding standards you want—details like indenting paragraphs or starting every chapter on a right-hand page. For each version you generate—Kindle, iBooks, Kobo, generic

.epub, and print—Vellum will give you a folder containing two files—the cover image and the formatted text.

It took me three passes at Kindle formatting before I was satisfied, and a couple more before I accepted the final print book layout. The learning curve is steep at first, but the results are pretty spectacular. The finished products appear to be attractive and indistinguishable from the quality produced by CreateSpace or Lightning Source. I intend to use this program on every book from now on. Vellum paid for itself before I finished creating my first print-ready file.

Remember that software, like underwear, does not come in one-size-fits-all. I enthusiastically recommended Scrivener to one and all when I started using it. One friend declared it a miracle of clarity and simplicity—the answer to all her problems. Another hated it, insisting that it was impossible to understand. No software fits everyone. Take the time to test the programs you hear about before you invest your money. Use whatever combination suits your own skill level and writing needs.

THE FIRST DRAFT

"Why NaNoWriMo May Not Be the Answer"

Lewis Carroll's Alice in Wonderland features two kinds of mice—the regular variety we all love and the dormouse, a mouse-like rodent with a fluffy tail. Both of them are into story-telling, and both do a terrible job of it. The first mouse, in chapter 3, tries to help Alice and her animal friends after they fall into her pool of tears. He offers them a lesson in English history since the story of William the Conqueror is the driest thing he knows. Then in chapter 7, we meet the Dormouse at the Mad Hatter's Tea Party. He sleeps in the teapot most of the time, but he launches himself into a sleepy story about three sisters who live in a treacle well and spend their time drawing pictures of things that begin with the letter M.

The first mouse makes fun of the kind of scholar who memorizes facts without thinking about them. The Dormouse's tale has not much of a beginning, no point, and shows no sign of ever ending, at least until the dormouse falls asleep again. Both are warnings about some of the ways a writer can stray if she begins to write without having a clear idea of what her story is all about.

Learning from Experience

National Novel Writing Month (fondly known among writers as NaNoWriMo) is an exercise in self-torture. Would-be writers sign up ahead of time but do not begin writing until the first day of November. For the next thirty days, they fall into a writing frenzy, the goal of which is to write at least 1,667 words every day. Instructions are to write without overthinking and to postpone all editing until after the month is over. November is for spilling words onto a page in the firm belief that at the end of the month, each writer will discover that those words have magically turned themselves into a novel of at least 50,000 words.

There are, of course, all sorts of flaws in that premise, starting with the fundamental truth that a length of 50,000 words is too short to qualify as a real novel. Still, writers accept the premise, and the NaNoWriMo organizers soothe any doubts by explaining that the author can always go back to add details later. The same applies to errors introduced any time fingers fly over keyboards faster than human minds can plot and plan. And perhaps there is some truth in the belief that once you have written 50,000 words, you will be committed to finishing the work you have started.

Thousands of writers all over the world sign up to be a part of this exercise. A dedicated website lets every participant keep a running total with a daily chart to illustrate progress. Coaches send out pep talks. Local group leaders organize get-togethers at libraries or coffee shops. A gift shop offers posters, stickers, tee shirts, coffee mugs, pens, and other souvenirs to commemorate the experience. And at the end, there are declared winners, with all writers who finish the goal receiving a certificate and banners to put on their websites.

In 2009, I decided to try this method of writing the first draft, and I did it. I finished two days ahead of schedule, which should have made me feel proud of myself. But if I'm honest, I have to admit I was not eager to go back and read what I had written. I had violated the rules left and right. An old English teacher cannot stand to see a spelling error and let it pass. I also backed up to correct silly details like whether a period belonged inside or outside a closing quotation mark. So I was pretty confident that what I produced was in passable English. But did it make sense? That was a whole different question.

My 50,000 words (50,626 to be exact) were the finishing chapters of a much longer novel that I had stopped writing in the middle. After letting it just sit there for six months, I signed up for NaNoWriMo, which forced me to jump in and finish the darn thing. I'd been feeling pretty smug ever since I completed the NaNoWriMo competition. The 50,000+ words I wrote nicely finished off my historical novel. I thought all I had left to do was polish it up a bit. Hah!

I had been working on the life story of a woman named Nellie Chase, who had an amazing experience as a Civil War nurse. Her story was compelling. She was a teenage runaway, the wife of a musician who turned out to be a drunkard, a liar, a gambler, a forger, and a thief. She escaped from his degrading lifestyle by signing up as a nurse with a Union regiment and traveling with them for a year. During that year she faced the usual hardships, compounded by a vengeful Presbyterian chaplain who thought she was a prostitute and by challenges to her understanding of what it would mean to put an end to slavery.

For that year, I had sufficient information in the form of letters from the members of the regiment, many of whom found her interesting enough to talk about at length. But I didn't know who Nellie was, or what happened to her after the war. That lack of information led me to turn her story into a novel, rather than a biography, and I had great fun creating a life for her before and after the war. NaNoWriMo was perfect for me. I had let my imagination fly and had created an exciting and plausible end to the story. So far so good!

Then one night in December I received an email from a friend who edits the website for the regiment in which Nellie served. He had found two small tidbits of information about her. One was a letter suggesting that Nellie was related to Salmon P. Chase, Lincoln's Secretary of the Treasury. The other was her obituary, listing the man she married after the war and relating the story of her heroic death during the Yellow Fever epidemic. My exciting and plausible ending was nowhere near as good as the real story. The truth, as often happens, was stranger than fiction.

It also meant that I had to discard much of what I had written in November, including all of my creative fantasies about what happened to Nellie after the war. So back to the records I went, armed with a new set of names and dates to be checked. It's a good thing I enjoy historical research. The historian in me was excited; the writer was a bit discouraged.

What's Wrong with Being a Pantser?

A year later I had re-written *Beyond All Price*, the story of Nellie Chase. The experience of speed writing had taught me to be more careful about what I wrote, but I still prided myself on being something of a pantser rather than a plotter. A pantser is someone whose story burns inside him. His characters insist on speaking out, and his writing happens by accident and surprise rather than because of some careful plan. He writes like a driver without a map, navigating by the seat of his pants. In contrast are the stodgy folks who sit down to map out a story before starting to write. Plotters write from a preconceived formula; pantsers write from inspiration—or so I thought.

I sneered at the very idea of becoming a plotter. Planning a book sounded both dull and lazy. The process reminded me of those half-hour sitcoms we all watch now and then as a pure escape. Viewers don't have to get involved with the characters because everyone knows in advance what will happen. Stock characters appear and reappear right on schedule. Each episode resolves itself within the same allotted time frame, with predictable results. How boring! How unoriginal!

By November 2010, I was ready to write a new book, and NaNoWriMo beckoned. Surely this time it would work. So how did my second venture into National Novel Writing Month turn out? Well, here's how I viewed it at the beginning of the process:

NaNoWriMo process was easier that year. I found I was better able to sit down and let the words flow. What was developing on my computer screen was by no means a finished product, but it would serve as a great base from which to build a real novel. I didn't think that *Gideon's Ladies* would write itself in a single month. The truth was, I knew I would still be reading and researching much of the time. I found it easiest to write dialogue, so I concentrated on creating scenes from various spots in the story. They could always be rearranged and polished later. As I wrote, I was getting a feel for the characters, and I found that some of the individuals had begun to speak in their own voices, which is always a delightful turning point. I was anxious to see what they were going to do next, and how they would handle the problems they had set for themselves.

By the end of the month, I was exhausted and not quite so sure of what I had managed to accomplish. After twenty-seven grueling days (actually twenty-five work days and two days of being a complete slacker) I had managed to write the first 50,417 words of my next novel. Was it worth it? Well, maybe. The writing phase is always hard, and putting a word counter on every morsel you manage to crank out is one definition of cruelty. But now I knew that this story had legs. It could someday become a novel, and when that day came, I would be delighted that I had spent November 2010 in this effort.

I dutifully sent my "winning" 50,000 words off to CreateSpace to take them up on their offer to produce a proof copy of every book that qualified as a winner at the end of the month. The thin little volume soon arrived—some 178 pages in all. I couldn't bear to look at it until after the holidays. Then I discovered it was pitiful. It was full of typos and half-finished pages, with thoughts that started off bravely and went nowhere.

I finally began re-reading *Gideon's Ladies*, but I was embarrassed by the number of mistakes and the layout. Once in a while I cringed. I had, however, learned a bit more about myself and the writing process. Here are five rules I was now willing to write on a rock:

- Don't start writing until you have some idea of where you're heading. These little chapters utterly failed to provide direction. An impartial reader could not tell who the leading characters were, or what the book was all about.
- Keep a timeline. My events were confusingly out of order.
- Don't confuse "show" and "tell." My academic

background revealed itself all too clearly when I fell into lecture mode. I thought I was writing conversations, but the result all too often sounded like a typical schoolmarm telling a class of students what they must know for the test. I wrote so quickly that I forgot to let my characters show what was going on through their words and actions.
- Know your characters. Each one needs a distinct personality, recognizable in both their actions and in their speech patterns. If the reader can't tell the characters apart, the author has failed again.
- Write because you have something important to say. The reader deserves to understand what is important about your story and why you care.

So where did I go from there? I made a start by changing my title from *Gideon's Ladies* (too over-used) to *The Road to Frogmore*. And that title reflected one other decision—to make Laura Towne and her efforts to establish her school at Frogmore Plantation the center of my story. My research efforts for the next several weeks focused on obeying my other new rules. I needed to fill out my character sketches, pinpointing those traits that made each character an individual. I needed to finish the timeline I had started so that the events of my story were both logical and historically accurate. Then I could re-arrange and refurbish some of the chapters I had written. Most importantly, I needed to make some decisions about point-of-view and recurring themes.

Herd Mentality May Not Be the Solution

As for NaNoWriMo, I did not participate in 2011. After my earlier experiences, I had decided that a November writing marathon was not for me. I had too many distractions that month—

travel plans, Thanksgiving, meeting commitments. On that crucial first day of November, I thought about writing a love letter to the participants.

All over the country on that crucial first day of November, bleary-eyed people dragged themselves out of bed and headed for their computers, intent on producing the next great American novel. I don't know how many would-be writers had signed up that year, but I estimated, based on previous years and advanced publicity, that there would be well over 200,000 participants. Can you even imagine how many words they would produce if all of them finished the challenge? By my count, ten billion. And how many complete novels? That's quite another issue.

I wished everyone well. I had done this exercise twice, and while I finished both times, I never produced anything that was publishable without several more months of work on it. But then, that's just my own experience. I noticed a lot of internet groups were doing build-ups to NaNoWriMo by practicing writing in spurts, as well as by plot outlining and character sketching. Technically, such preparation is against the rules, but it will undoubtedly help those who would otherwise spend most of the month hunting for a story.

Maybe one year, someone actually will produce the next great American novel using this method. I suspect, however, that the real accomplishment will be something else. Almost everyone I talk to wants to write a book some day. Taking part in NaNoWriMo is a great way to discover if writing is really for you. Thirty days at the computer, cranking out a minimum of 1667 words every day? If you find you like it, if you start writing more than the minimum, if you find that you are becoming wrapped up in your story, then maybe writing is a career to consider. If all you get out of it is frustration, a pile of undone laundry and dirty dishes, and a raging case of fanny fatigue, then you'll know that it's time to take up another hobby, like snowshoe hiking or tatting a rug. Either way, it will be time well-spent.

If things go well, the phone won't ring, the plumbing won't clog, no one will get sick, and all writers will experience waves of inspiration that translate into glowing prose. I would be rooting for every participant—just doing it from the sidelines in 2011.

Why? When I looked at my previous year's writing in print, I saw every flaw. But I could also see where I had gone wrong and what I needed to do to correct it. So with an awful example before me, I started over, asked myself the right questions, and eventually published *The Road to Frogmore*, a much-improved version that allowed me to take the time I needed to develop each step.

A Different Approach

As my writing methods changed, and as I learned more about the whole process, so did NaNoWriMo. They added smaller versions of their contests in April and July. These camp-like experiences were more like writing retreats. Authors found themselves in virtual cabins, where the organizers matched them with others working on the same sorts of materials. The program kept track of each camper's progress but added the combined word counts for each cabin. Cabin-mates could chat with each other, talk about writing problems, or ask for help. Writers were also allowed to set their own word-count goals, which relaxed some of the pressure.

April or July suited me much better. Yes, despite a pledge never to do one of these marathons again, I decided that I needed to do something drastic to jump-start my next book. April writing camp seemed promising because they let us set our own goals this time. Mine started out at 35,000 words.

I wrote every day, except for the weekend of April 18-19, when I was away managing a two-day meeting of the non-profit for which I served as president. On April 28, I topped out at 37,244 words, although there were two days left in the month. I had written a significant portion of *Damned Yankee* in April 2013.

Do I recommend this approach? Yes and no. This time, it worked for me, and I was looking at the first forty percent or so of my next book. Even better, when I read over what I had churned out, it sounded pretty good. I learned a lot along the way. My characters took over and changed the story a bit. They also changed the title about half way through.

Part of the secret is that NaNoWriMo encourages you to sit down and pound out the words without overthinking it too much. You're not supposed to worry about spelling or typos. All those corrections come later. It's the story that is most important. I have trouble ignoring my typos, particularly because the character T on my keyboard sticks and I keep leaving that letter out. Still, it had been a fun exercise, and now I was energized and ready to go on with the rest of the book.

The More Preparation the Better

In July 2015 I wrote the final section of *Yankee Reconstructed* in another NaNoWriMo summer cabin. Go ahead. Call me an idiot. Label this as a failure of a twelve-step addiction cure. I know I swore I would never do another one of these masochistic writing marathons that made me hate myself. But there I was again, needing something—anything—to push me over the final hurdles to the end of *Yankee Reconstructed*.

My goal for the book had always been to finish it at approximately 100,000 words. By the summer of 2015, I had written 78,704 words, which put me at the 79% finished mark. Only 21,296 to go, although you understand (particularly if you're a writer) that I would need more than that when I got to the editing and pruning stage of the manuscript. The usual goal for a participant in NaNoWriMo is 50,000 words, so I set my own goals much lower than normal. If I managed to write 800 words a day for July, I would have finished the first draft of the book.

Could I do 800 words a day? Sure! Easy, provided I managed to get the seat of my pants into the seat of the chair every day. But that was the problem, of course. It was summer, and my office was hot and stuffy. There were other things I'd rather be doing. I was covering some unfamiliar territory by the time I reached 1876, so I needed research breaks. I promised to work the Lions Fishing Rodeo on the 4th of July. A friend wanted to meet for lunch. You've heard the excuses before, and you'll hear them again. But somehow, I was determined to make myself do this. And if all the silliness and hype of NaNoWriMo helped me do it, GREAT!

As June came to an end, I went to the grocery store to stock up on Hershey's Kisses, which would become my rewards. I laid in a supply of frozen lunch entrees so that I won't be tempted to go off on some wild cooking spree in the middle of my writing day. I checked the house and replenished supplies of toilet paper, Kleenex, bottled water, toothpaste, cat food, stamps, printer cartridges, sticky notes, and colored pens. I was not taking any chances on being lured away by a desperate need for one of life's essential elements.

I cleaned the house (well, most of it!), tossed out some penicillin-producing left-overs, and paid all the bills. I pulled the weeds and dead blossoms off my little row of front porch planters, and poured this month's supply of baking soda, vinegar, and boiling water down the drains to make sure they didn't clog up on me. Then I tackled my writing office, blowing away the month's accumulation of cat fur, emptying the trash, picking up cat toys, finding all my vital reference books, and bringing my new July calendar up to date with the deadlines I had set myself.

What else did I need before the marathon started? Well, the NaNoWriMo camp counselors would be assigning me to my writers' cabin, and I was eager to learn who my cabin-mates (competitors) would be. These were the people to whom I would report each day as we strove to see who could get the most done. The last time I did this, I ended up in a cabin full of silly teenagers writing werewolf fantasies. They all got homesick (or bored) and gave up after the first week. This time I asked for cabin-mates of people my age or other writers of historical fiction.

Some Things They Don't Tell You

I've uncovered two underlying fault lines in that rock-hard theory that a writer can sit down every day for a month—any month—and churn out a set number of words—with the result that a book miraculously appears at the end of thirty days. Oh, there are any number of people who will tell you they've done it (Hey, I've done it!), and there are book publishers out there who are ready to turn those random words into printed pages. Sure there are.

BUT—there has to be a but. One problem comes from the assumption that the Muse is always on call. Often, she is. I have those days when the characters grab my story line and start talking to themselves in my head as fast as I can hit the keys. And if I'm interrupted—a neighbor drops by, an urgent request arrives in e-mail, or the cat food runs out, I can stop typing and take care of the problem without interrupting my line of thought. I can empty the dishwasher or fix a light bulb or take out the garbage while the characters keep right on talking in my head.

Yes, yes, don't bother telling me. I know that's another one of those bad signs—like drinking my coffee black or craving radishes—that proves I'm a psychopath at heart. That's all right. It's those voices that help a writer write.

On other days, the same characters stick their noses in the air, fold their arms across their chests, turn their backs, and refuse to utter a word. And when they do that, there's no real cure. Any attempt to write while the Muse is on strike produces nothing but drivel.

The other fault line is life itself. The creators of NaNoWriMo sometimes seem to have forgotten that Life with a capital L is no respecter of the plans of ordinary mortals. Things happen. The power goes out. The computer crashes. Some clumsy four-footed monster knocks a glass off the kitchen counter and leaves hundreds of sharp splinters underfoot. And sometimes the distraction is something delightful. A friend receives a prestigious award and invites you to attend the award celebration. A long-distance call reawakens another friendship. Whether they be welcome or not, some interruptions put an end to a whole day's production schedule.

My July 2015 attempt produced some good work, and I foolishly decided to use the regular NaNoWriMo challenge in November to do a thorough edit of the manuscript. Disasters followed. My word count fell far short of the goal, and once more, I vowed never to do it again.

New Plan: Plot, Then Apply Seat of Pants to Chair

Camp NaNoWriMo was almost here for April 2017! Just two more days before we hit the keyboards. And I was almost ready. My camp shirt hung in the closet. My Scrivener files were set up with a chapter-by-chapter tentative outline of *Henrietta's Journal*, character sketches, a few pictures that showed the period, a historical timeline, and a collection of articles on relevant historical events. The opening chapters were written (in first draft form). Now I was looking ahead, hoping to complete the 50,000 to 70,000 words it would take to finish an early draft of this new manuscript. Could I do it? Who knows? But I was going to try. I've been in this business long enough to know that nothing works as well as just applying the seat of pants to the computer chair, particularly when the preliminary work is complete.

One of the interesting highlights of doing the April or June Camp NaNoWriMo experience is the casual atmosphere. Participants write, but they also toast some imaginary marshmallows and exchange scary stories with the other campers. The program assigns us to cabins, in which we get to know ten or twelve other campers. I asked to be assigned to a cabin with other writers of historical fiction, and then, hopeful to the end, to people who were close to my age. The last times I did this, you'll remember, my cabins contained some thirteen-year-olds who became sidetracked and disappeared after only a few days. My match-ups this year were much better, although it's hard to find other writers in their late 70s. So my cabin held mostly those who wanted to write historical novels. We had three or four other retired women, several in their mid to late thirties, and a few who wouldn't talk about their age (maybe that's a giveaway!). Four of us had already published; the others were still neophytes.

We had a virtual bulletin board where we could share ideas, doubts, questions, and mutually helpful ideas. Several of our newcomers had already expressed some anxiety about two areas—not knowing what to write and wondering about the possibilities of self-publishing. Their questions spurred me to jump in with comments. I knew I could be of help in both areas.

Could I finish the first draft of a novel in thirty days? Sure I could! As a group, our cabin was lucky, too. Several completed their goals while others expressed their satisfaction at how much they had been able to accomplish. This latest NaNoWriMo experience confirmed my suspicions:

- Speed-writing without direction is time wasted.
- Pantsers usually end up going back to do the plotting they skipped.
- Support groups encourage continued efforts.
- No one else should set an arbitrary word-count goal for you.
- Motivation matters. You have to want to write.
- You need periods of concentrated effort interspersed with frequent breaks.

But what was it that made a difference for me in 2017? I had given up my long-cherished notions of being a pantser. I was never going to be the kind of author whose books sprang to life fully formed from some inner source of inspiration. No, I had become a planner. I had worked out a story line, a group of fleshed-out characters, and a couple of themes I wanted to follow. I was ready to write because I knew what I wanted to say.

Write it on a rock: Don't start your writing journey until you know where you are headed.

PLANNING THE BOOK

"¡Arriba, Arriba! ¡Ándale, Ándale!"

If you grew up watching Looney Tunes, you'd recognize the cry of Speedy Gonzales, the fastest mouse in all of Mexico. Speedy Gonzales doesn't get a whole lot of play these days, and we see him as an unfortunate stereotype, but in his heyday, everyone knew his character, his legendary speed and agility, and his ongoing battle with Sylvester the Cat. Speedy was always the hero, and he always had a goal—to rescue some hapless creature from certain disaster. The arch-villain, of course, was Sylvester, who was out to thwart Speedy's efforts. And the story moved from crisis to crisis, each one more dangerous than the last, until Sylvester fell victim to Speedy's clever schemes. The dastardly plot failed, and Speedy reigned as the conquering hero, at least until the next cartoon episode.

If you can forgive him his ridiculous Mexican accent, you'll recognize Speedy Gonzales as the classic action hero in a thriller. And without the sombrero and the red bandana, he can serve you as an effective guide for plotting your next story. You must have a main character. That character must have a goal. Something or someone must stand in the way of reaching that goal. And the suspense must escalate until the story reaches a satisfying conclusion. So what's holding you back? *¡Ándale, ándale!*

How Do You Create a Plot?

There are probably as many answers to that question as there are books in print. Here's how I did it, but remember, this is just one approach. The story of the Gideonites and the Port Royal Experiment had no lack of colorful characters. It was full of fascinating people. It had all kinds of exotic scenery—swamps, pluff mud, tropical vegetation, glorious sunrises, sandy ocean beaches. It had drama—a background of America's Civil War, heroic acts of bravery, enormous pain and suffering, and a life-changing struggle for freedom. Why, then, couldn't I make any progress with the book? The answer is right here, in this very paragraph. The story was simply too big to handle.

But, oh, how hard it is to cut out all those great tidbits. I had what amounted to half a book already written—some 50,000 words

I had created during the previous year's National Novel Writing Month. The chapters were just sitting there, waiting, but I couldn't tell where they were going next. I started cutting hunks of extraneous material out of those chapters. The remaining 35,000 words were more coherent than the first version, but the direction was still unclear.

Eventually, of course, I recognized my errors. I was writing like a historian. Now, there's nothing wrong with being a historian. It's what I am by training and experience. I want to know what happened, why it happened, who all was involved, when and where it happened (all the usual journalist's questions), as well as the nature of the underlying causes and results. All are legitimate questions. All are important. All call for more research. And none of them has much to do with the structure of a novel.

The light clicked on first while I was reading a discussion about creating a press release. "Summarize your plot in a single sentence. Then expand it to two sentences. Make the reader want to know what's going to happen." I couldn't do it—because I didn't have a plot. I was just describing events, hoping that they would magically arrange themselves into an acceptable story. So far, they weren't showing any signs of being able to do that on their own. So I had 35,000 words, but they didn't make the beginning of a novel.

For a novel, I had to build a plot, one with a definite beginning, a middle, and an end. It needed a theme, a message, a reason for its existence. It required one main character—someone with a back story, a character with an appealing personality but a few personal quirks, a character with whom the reader could identify. That character had to have a goal that was important not only to her but the reader, and she needed an adversary that stood in the way of reaching that goal. The story needed to provide tension, a crisis (or two or three), and a resolution that would be not necessarily happy but reasonable in the light of all that went before.

The solution was obvious but too drastic to contemplate. Instead of just trashing the project, I stepped away from it for a while and sought a guru—someone who could tell me what to do to salvage the idea. I started by reading an excellent book: *Story Engineering* by Larry Brooks. He offered a step by step guide for building the underlying structure of a novel. As I read, I kept a notepad at hand, where I scratched out ideas of how I could take my historical knowledge and mold it into a workable plot outline. And somehow my story did arrange itself. Once I had the main structural elements in place, the people, the places, and the events made sense.

The 35,000 words? Trashed! The book itself? Rejuvenated!

Killing My Darlings

The next step involved a scrutiny of my cast of characters. I asked myself a couple of questions. Whose story drives *The Road to Frogmore*? Which character is most affected by the events? Which one has the most to lose? I soon recognized that the primary focus should fall on Laura Towne, the founder of the Penn Center on St. Helena Island. And at that point I had to launch into a rampage of murder and mayhem. When I listed all the names of real people with whom Laura came in contact during her first years in South Carolina, there turned out to be hundreds of them—and most of those had to go.

I examined both individuals and groups, always asking the same question: *Did this person help or hinder Laura in a meaningful way?* I kept the character if the answer was yes. But if I could not make a case for individuals as significant, I killed their characters, no matter how fascinating their personal stories seemed. Here are some of my victims.

The members of the Roundhead Regiment, including Nellie Chase and her small family of ex-slaves, were dear to me because I knew them well. They were in Beaufort when Laura arrived. They met on several occasions. Laura and Nellie had a few similar slave encounters. But there is no evidence that Nellie and company influenced Laura in any way. That they reached somewhat similar conclusions about slavery speaks only to the validity of their discoveries. Although I have had readers of *A Scratch with the Rebels* and *Beyond All Price* ask for more, these characters had already lived their moments in the sun. This new book was not their story.

Robert Smalls lived an influential life. He had a connection with Laura's group of Gideonites because his wife and children worked at Coffin Point, the plantation run by Edward Philbrick. Laura often visited, bringing medical care to the freedmen there, and when Smalls pulled off his great act of derring-do, I'm sure Laura was among those who cheered him. But while others of the Gideonites hustled Smalls off to Washington to show that a slave could do great things for the country, his accomplishments had no permanent effect on Laura or the children in Laura's classroom. My book was not about his story, either.

Who has not heard of Harriet Tubman, a plucky little black woman from Maryland, who led escaped slaves along the Underground Railroad, penetrated Confederate lines to spy for the United States, and led a raid into the interior of South Carolina to rescue slaves and bring them to safety in the Low Country? Laura knew her and admired her. Harriet certainly made an impact on St. Helena Island when she turned up leading over seven hundred newly freed slaves, hoping that someone would house them, feed them, and teach them what they needed to know. But did her actions influence Laura and her ability to achieve her goal? Not really. Harriet Tubman deserves books of her own. My story is not one of them.

The Gideonites themselves formed a fascinating group of characters. A total of seventy-three people traveled to South Carolina in the spring of 1862, all determined in one way or another to prove the rightness of the abolitionist cause. They were socialites and sheltered spinsters, old and young, teachers, ministers, lawyers, philanthropists, and failed merchants. And all of them had back stories that explained why they gave up almost everything to risk this venture. The spiritual leader of the group found himself on trial as a kleptomaniac because he was hopeless at bookkeeping. The opera singer with seven children wrote such lurid prose that it was almost pornographic. The cotton agent beat one of the other Gideonites to a battered and bloody wreck. The wealthy socialite could not lower herself to do actual work of any kind. By being both teacher and black, the free mulatto woman confounded everyone who expected to see a color separation between teachers and students. How could I ignore them?

The Gideonites as a group were worthy of study, and as individuals, their stories made great reading. Once again, my reasons for choosing to feature some of them and ignore others depended on the impact they had on Laura and her goal. If they played a crucial role in the plot, they stayed. If they went home early or had little or nothing to contribute to the main story, I reduced them to the status of bit players or sent them away entirely.

And what about the former slaves themselves? There were hundreds of them, and without them, Laura's reason for coming to South Carolina disappeared. Each of them had a tale to tell, as Austa the Pornographer discovered. But to focus on each one of them would be impossible. Instead, I chose to focus on one strong black woman who could speak for all of them. She could be present for the whole story. She could comment on events and tell the stories that the others could not pass on. Think of her as a one-woman black chorus, speaking for all of the enslaved.

The All-Important Character Sketch

Once you have chosen your main characters, you'll need to get to know them before you can write about them. Taking the time to build a character sketch for each of your individuals will help you to bring them alive in your reader's imagination. It will also save you from making detail blunders such as changing a character's eye-color half way through the story or owning a cat at the beginning and a dog later on. Here are some ways to meet your heroes and villains.

I find that compiling a character sketch of each person is an indispensable first step. To my delight, I discovered that newer versions of Scrivener provide a template for such sketches. (If you are not familiar with Scrivener, the best writing software available, you owe it to yourself to check it out at http://www.literatureandlatte.com/scrivener.php). The template offers the following sections: role in the story, occupation, physical description, personality, habits and mannerisms, background, internal conflicts, external conflicts, and notes.

Here are some of the resources I use to compile this information for my works of historical fiction.

Since most of my characters are real people, I start with a general history text that describes the events I intend to include. Plundering the index is a quick way to identify such details as a character's occupation and background.

My second resource is usually the U. S. Census. Any good genealogy program can quickly find any listing of the character in whom you are interested. I concentrated on such things as the family's economic status and my individual's place within the household. Among the women I considered as main characters in *The Road to Frogmore*, I found one who was the only girl in a huge family of boys—thus explaining, perhaps, why so many people commented on her masculine habits and interests. Another was a nine-year-old-child when her mother died, leaving her to help raise four younger brothers and sisters. No need to wonder where she developed her nurturing nature.

Photographs can reveal much. One of my ladies was a spinster. Her students adored her, but many of the men around her treated her as an object of scorn. Why? Well, a single glance at her only formal portrait drew my attention to her unfortunately huge bulbous nose.

The character's writings—letters, diaries, journals, other publications—complete the picture. One of my characters was a preacher's wife. I knew she was a singer and a teacher, as well as the leading force among the evangelical abolitionists. I didn't fully understand her, however, until I discovered the book she had written about the evils of slavery. It revealed her to be not only an intemperate zealot but a lascivious one at that. I might have missed that part of her character if I had not taken the time to compile a character sketch.

The template works equally well for fantasy, purely fictional characters, historical figures, and even the people involved in historical monographs. You must know your character very well before you can expect your reader to understand and identify with him.

Speed - Dating

Most writing guides will devote a chapter or more to characterization. They offer good advice. Make the people in your novel believable. Avoid stereotypes, which are, by definition, boring. A talkative librarian is more interesting than a sternly silent one. And a neatly-dressed plumber might be fascinating merely because of what you don't see when he bends over. Don't force a character to perform superhuman feats, unless, of course, you're into writing fantasy. Reveal personalities a bit at a time. Don't overwhelm the reader with lengthy descriptions at the very beginning. Let the reader get to know your characters gradually, in much the same way as you get to know real people in your life. It's all good advice. But how do you do all that?

One way is to imagine your characters in a speed-dating setting. Visualize each one sitting across from you. You have only a few minutes to decide if you like or distrust them. You're taking notes so that you can remember them later. Besides recording hair and eye color, height and weight, ask each of them a series of questions:

- What is your name? Does it have a special significance to your family? Do you have a nickname?
- How old are you, and where were you born? Have you stayed in one location or moved around? And if you have moved, at what point in your life?
- What was your family like when you were growing up? Did you have brothers and sisters, and where do you fall, age-wise, in the list of your parents' children? Are you still the responsible one because you were the oldest? Or are you the forgotten middle child, or the spoiled youngest one?
- Did you have pets as a child? If you could choose just one pet, would you turn out to be a cat-person (independent) or a dog-person (eager and friendly)?
- Do you have a large circle of companions or only a couple of close friends? Have you moved in the same small circle all your life, or have you reached out to meet new people? And how do you choose your friends?
- What is your greatest strength? Your biggest weakness?
- What do you dream of doing? If you could be someone else, who would you choose to be?
- What beliefs do you hold most tightly? Which ones would you be willing to write on a rock?
- What is your idea of a perfect day? Where and with whom would you spend it, and what would you do?
- Why do you dress the way you do? Are you usually neat or disheveled? Are you stylish or old-fashioned? Are you uncomfortable in a suit and tie—or in high heels and a fancy dress?
- What are your favorite expressions? Do you use the

latest slang, or do you show off your extensive vocabulary? Do you slip into a more pronounced accent or dialect when you are excited? Do you have a verbal tic, saying "um" or "uh" or "like" or "you know?"
- What does your posture say about you? Do you slouch, or hunch your shoulders, or keep your arms crossed? Do you keep your eyes on the ground when you walk? Or are your shoulders thrown back as a sign of confidence?
- What about eye contact? Do you keep looking away, or are you giving me a hostile stare? Are you squinting at me or raising a skeptical eyebrow? Are you avoiding eye contact because you are nervous or because you are bored? Does your smile reach your eyes?
- Does standing close to someone make you uncomfortable? Or do you frequently reach out to make physical contact?
- And what do your other gestures say about you? Do you play with your hair or brush it back impatiently? Do you have a twitch or unconscious mannerism? Do you pick at a hangnail, chew your lip, shuffle your feet, or bite your fingernails?

We all send out signals with our body language, and most of us can interpret those signals, if only subconsciously. If your characters behave as real people do, your readers will judge them accordingly.

Understanding Point of View

You can't figure out how to get to where you're going until you know your starting point. That may sound like a formula for a travel column, but it applies equally well to the design of a book. It also applies similarly to the writer and to the reader. It's called establishing a point of view. If an author has not decided on the point of view, the resulting book will wander around from character to character without focus. And if the reader cannot recognize the point of view, the story will make little sense.

There are five points of view from which to choose:

First-Person—This is the classic "I" narrative. The author seems to be telling the story, although it may or may not have happened. This point of view lends itself best to memoirs, "tell-all" revelations, or psychological thrillers. It is also the natural choice for the contents of a diary. In fact, I have just finished writing a historical novel that consists entirely of the main character's journal entries. It does, however, impose limitations on the narrative, which can only contain facts the speaker or writer is in a position to know. He may record a conversation, but he cannot know what is going through the other person's mind.

Second-Person—This is the "You" position, which tries to draw the reader into participating in the story. The approach can become awkward in practice, but it can also be used effectively if the writer wants to make the reader experience the full panoply of emotions in a situation.

Third-Person-Limited—Each character knows only his or her reactions or experiences. The character can engage in a conversation, but the reader only knows what he is thinking, not what both participants have in mind. In practice that can be a bit tricky to pull off.

Third-Person-Omniscient—In this case, the author knows what is going on in everyone's mind, which can be very confusing if there are many characters in a story. It is, however, a frequently used point of view because it allows the author to have great power over the characters.

Mixed-Point-of-View—The most important character narrates her own experiences, while separate sections in third-person reveal what else is happening. The constantly shifting point of view can be confusing to the reader unless the author takes care to label each chapter so that the viewpoint remains clear.

Whose Story Is this, Anyway?

The decision to make a slave woman a major character presented a new problem regarding the point of view. Laura Towne was not yet in the Low Country when some of the crucial events took place. In almost every case, the slaves were the ones whose lives were being turned upside down. But could I write the story from the slaves' point of view? That would be a real stretch, for a couple of reasons.

First, there is almost no evidence of what the slaves thought about the goings on in South Carolina during the Civil War. It would be accurate to say they were confused, I suppose, but there is no evidence to back up even that claim. It was against state law for slaves to learn to read or write, so there are few extant letters or diaries. The slaves spoke the Gullah language among themselves, so the first whites who came to work with them found them almost unintelligible. With no record of what they thought, I would be unwilling to trust my creative ability to fictionalize their attitudes.

Second, the slaves were not in a position to understand much of what was going on around them. Even if we could find some record of their reactions, they were limited because no one had ever taught them about politics, or military strategy, or religious differences. Some of them had heard about Baby Jesus and Uncle Sam, but they had no real understanding of those concepts. Their white masters had wanted to keep them as ignorant as possible because a lack of knowledge prevented them from rising in revolt. No, the slaves would not do as the narrators of my story.

And yet, I needed to understand the story from their point of view! As I struggled to deal with this issue, I realized that I did have a bit of evidence about the slaves after all. In the Laura Towne diary and letters, Laura made repeated references to Rina, the woman who did her laundry and ironing for a small salary. Rina held a high place in the slave matriarchy, evidenced by the fact that when the slaves assembled for a Shout, they did so at Rina's cabin. Laura, too, found that Rina was invaluable. The diary echoed with one phrase — "Rina tells me that . . ." Rina already functioned as something of a one-woman Greek chorus, commenting on the events of the day and the foolishness of the people around her. As trust built up between the two women, Rina became Laura's window into the world of the slaves.

Once I understood Rina's role in my story, the decision about the point of view was apparent. This book would use a mixed point of view, except for the sections devoted to Rina. Rina's comments and stories would appear in short chapters written in the first person. Laura's diary provided a close enough approximation to allow me to record Rina's own words, and I wanted to let her speak for herself. But she could not discuss all the ideological differences that erupted into crisis points in the story. Since she did not understand what the cotton agents were trying to accomplish, their part of the story must appear in a third-person narrative. The same was true of the soldiers and the missionaries who came to South Carolina from a variety of backgrounds and with diverse motives.

Because there were many stories, I used a mixed third person point of view for all of the characters except Rina. Each chapter designated the character who appeared as the subject of that chapter. Switching the point of view allowed the reader to relate to one character at a time as the focus shifted to those who were most affected by events at any given moment.

The result, I hope, allows the reader a clearer understanding of what the Gideonite Experiment was all about. When Rina speaks, she knows what her experience has taught her. She may make assumptions about the other characters, but she is presenting a personal opinion. She speaks her mind, allowing the reader to understand her, even if the truths she speaks are unwelcome.

When the book turns to the people who surround Rina, the third person point of view allows the reader to form his own opinion about each of the characters because it offers many views.

And that, I think, is the real message of the book. It presents as dispassionately as possible the ideological clashes that divided people during the Civil War. It does not choose between North and South, Evangelical and Unitarian, abolitionist and slave owner, civilian and soldier, businessman and humanitarian, states rights advocate and federalist. But the one constant feature is the voice of Rina, reminding the reader that she was the one with the most to lose if the world made the wrong choices.

The Challenge of the Touchy Subject

The next step in re-designing the new book was to identify the theme or message. I identified two major ideas that affected almost every part of my story. Both of them were controversial.

The first had to do with the Abolitionists as a group. They talked about the evils of slavery, the need for emancipation, and the potential for turning slaves into loyal and productive citizens. I know Laura herself agreed with every one of those points. But what the Gideonites didn't seem to recognize was the degree to which they harbored some level of prejudice against the blacks. They wanted the slaves freed but still saw them as a working class. They paid them a small salary for their labor, but needed them to keep working at the same jobs they had always done. They observed the religious practices that went on in the slave cabins—the Shout, for example—and labeled them heathenish. They complained that the blacks were no longer obedient. They wanted to change their child-raising practices, their marriage customs, their level of cleanliness, their dress. They wanted to free the blacks and then turn them into whites. But they did not expect them to rise to the abolitionists' level of personhood.

Laura was as guilty of these attitudes as any of them, but she did struggle against them. In several places in her diary, she marveled at incidents in which she forgot the issue of race. Two black school teachers visited her one day, and at dinner, the conversation was exciting and stimulating as they discussed the methods that worked well in the classroom. Later she wrote that she enjoyed the evening so much that she failed to notice that the two visitors were black.

How will readers react to such incidents? Will they feel uncomfortable about being reminded that even the best of us have prejudices against those who are different? Are my readers going to see this theme as polemic? I assume that people more or less expect a Civil War novel to deal with racial issues. Of course, it does, and the revelation that even the staunchest abolitionist was not completely color blind may not be particularly shocking.

But there was another issue that lay beneath my entire story, one that dealt with gender roles. Laura Towne had a friend, Ellen Murray. They were (take your pick): best friends, life-long companions, partners, intimate friends, soul mates. People have applied all those terms to these two women who left their families and fled to South Carolina to establish a household and work together toward a common cause. They lived together for forty years, remaining faithful to one another to the exclusion of all others until death parted them.

I have been unable to find any overt mention of a sexual relationship between the two women, but given the repressive nature of nineteenth-century mores, that is not surprising. Not even long-married couples talked about sex in the 1860s. But there are intense emotional moments. Laura fears that Ellen will not be able to join her and faints with relief when Ellen arrives. The two greet each other with restraint and then "cavort with glee" when they are finally alone. Laura is at one spot struck dumb by Ellen's fragile beauty. Ellen believes her purpose in life is to take care of Laura. The crisis points in Laura's story frequently have to do with Ellen.

Changes in their relationship send their story off in new directions. It becomes impossible to talk about one without the other.

The relationship has gone undefined by historians. I suspect that is at least in part because of our own societal disagreements about same-sex marriages and partnerships. In the nineteenth century, there was a conventional family structure known as a Boston marriage. Even gender studies experts disagree about the exact nature of the relationship, but it always seems to involve two unrelated women living together as husband and wife, thus forming a family unit. Is this what was going on between Laura and Ellen?

Could I ignore this issue in the book? I didn't think I could. I don't want to get into a whole discussion about gender issues here. However, if Laura and Ellen were a part of a gender-based minority—if they experienced discrimination because of their affection for one another—then that might help explain why they chose to build their life together in the isolation of the Sea Islands rather than the urban settings of their upbringings. Their experience with discrimination may also have given them empathy for the problems faced by the freed slaves.

The Story Arc

Once you have figured out your main characters, determined the point of view, and identified a general theme or two, you come back to the crucial question. How do you lay out the events and details so that they pull the readers into the heart of the story and keep them turning pages until the end? I frequently suggest that writers having trouble coming up with a story line should spend a little time watching hour-long TV dramas. If you don't have time for that, think about a favorite children's book or nursery rhyme. "The Three Little Pigs" serves the purpose well.

The first requirement is that the story must have a hero. Then the hero needs to have a goal, and there must be a villain trying to keep him from reaching that goal. The Three Little Pigs are the heroes. They are cute as can be, all chubby and pink, so that we are sure to like them. Their goal is finding a home that will assure their survival. The villain is the Big Bad Wolf who moves into the neighborhood because, unfortunately, he likes pork. (This is the inciting incident.)

Trouble soon erupts. Pig #1 builds a house (his solution), although his choice of grass as the building material is pretty weak. The first hero's attempt to overcome the danger and reach the goal fails, as the villain thwarts his plans. The Big Bad Wolf comes along and blows it away. (Crisis #1 is serious, but it can be overcome.)

Faced with the knowledge of what happened to the first attempt, the second hero must try to find a better solution. When it also fails, tensions will increase. Pig #2 builds a better house, using sticks this time (recovery from the crisis), but the Big Bad Wolf crashes it quickly. (Crisis #2 ratchets up the tension.)

Now the story has reached the point of no return. If the third hero cannot come up with a final solution, they are doomed.

Pig #3 steps up and builds his house of bricks, which is an excellent solution to their problem. The Big Bad Wolf can't destroy it from the outside, so he crawls onto the roof to stomp it in. If this house doesn't survive, our pigs are indeed doomed. (Crisis #3 has us holding our breath.)

The reader waits to learn the outcome, fearing the worst. Then the Big Bad Wolf falls down the chimney and lands in a pot of water boiling on the fire. The climax is something of a miracle, but, hey, this is a fairy tale!

And now we can wrap up the story with a gradual feel-good letdown. The Three Little Pigs throw a few veggies into the pot, and they all feast on wolf stew for dinner before living happily ever after. (The usual denouement for a fairy tale.)

The Formula Every Writer Needs to Understand

Now let's go back to that TV drama you've been watching. You'll find the same elements, although they may be a bit more subtle than our "Three Little Pigs" episode. (Or maybe not.)

There will be a hero, although she may be a heroine, or a group of people, like a SWAT team or the NCIS crew. But even if there are several heroes, they will all have the same goal (saving the patient, getting the bad guy, preventing an accident or crime, winning the court case).

There must be a villain like a serial killer or a deranged knife-waving maniac, although the villain may not be a human being at all. Think about a bomb primed to explode, an epidemic threatening a city, a dangerous storm heading their way, a gang of crooks targeting old folks, a corrupt political machine, or even a war.

Once the audience has met the heroes and villains, there will come an inciting incident, the first clue that we have a problem. And suddenly it's time for a commercial, probably about ten or fifteen minutes into the program. Why now? Because you have invested time in the story, you like the good guys, and you want to know how they will handle the threat. You're not likely to change the channel—or close the book.

When we return to the program, the solution is relatively quick and easy. Whew! There may even be a bit of comic relief or human interest. But the relief is short-lived because a greater crisis occurs, one that ratchets up the danger level. Whoops! Another commercial break comes at the halfway point, to give you time to worry about the outcome.

That pattern will recur at least once, or maybe several times, but if you're paying close attention, you'll see that each crisis is worse than the one that came before it. The danger and the tension rise. More ads? Probably.

The Point of No Return will come when there are only a few more minutes left in the show. The bomb expert is ready to cut the wire. The surgeon hovers over the tumor with his scalpel. The cops enter the room where the murderer awaits them. The jury returns with a verdict. And we pause to bring you another ad because there's no way you're leaving now!

And then comes the conclusion, wrapped up in as few words as possible. There's an emotional reaction, a final explosion or gunshot, and it's all over. You'll see the pattern repeated over and over again on your favorite shows, but you'll keep coming back to watch every week, secure in the knowledge that the good guys will win in the end.

And yes, books work in the same way, although they may take longer to tell the story and there are no advertising breaks. But if you understand the pattern, you'll spot the critical events just as quickly. Chapter breaks can often work like commercials.

Does that mean other writers have already told all the stories? Is there just one story? Of course not. There are innumerable variations; every story is different. Do you have to follow the formula? No, you can do what you like. But your readers will expect you to follow the rules, and you ignore them at your peril.

DOING YOUR HOMEWORK

"There's a rat in my soup."

The Tale of Despereaux by Kate DiCamillo is one of my all-time favorite children's books. Despereaux is a mouse born with several distinguishing marks. He is tiny, but his ears are huge, giving him a keen sense of hearing. His eyes, open at birth, are yellow, and his nose is red. He is weak and helpless, so instead of doing the usual mousey things, he dreams of great adventures. With those big ears, he spends his time listening to everything going on around him. His wide-open eyes lead him to read books rather than eat them—books about heroic knights who save beautiful princesses from being trapped in castle dungeons. And from his reading and from his ability to hear what others miss, he learns how to be courageous in the face of such dangers as having his tail cut off by the cook, or ending up in prison because another rodent poisoned the queen's soup.

Despereaux sets a perfect example for anyone who plans to write a book. He listens, observes, reads, and dreams of great adventures. And at last the day comes when he can put all the things he has learned to work as he sets out to rescue his own Princess Pea. Does this mean that you are ready to write? Not so fast. First, you have a lot of homework to do.

Doing the Research

As a writer, I have a streak of perversity. No, I'm not into kinky sex scenes or ghoulish fantasy. My brand of perversity is yielding to the temptation to write something far removed from my assigned topic.

When I was in grad school, just starting to work on my dissertation, I was fascinated by the character of the Norman bishop whose career I was supposed to be studying. I had 134 of his letters to provide satisfaction for my curiosity. To me, the bishop was the type of fellow one loves to hate. I knew I couldn't believe a thing he said. He didn't call what he did lying, I suppose. He just told every person whatever they wanted to hear. So he was perfectly capable of telling the king that his son was plotting against him. Then he could turn around and offer the prince his help in overthrowing his father. He was a hypochondriac, inherently lazy, overly interested in his wealth, and a complete coward when danger threatened. What a great villain he would have made! I could have had a wonderful romp telling his story.

Opposing my views was my dissertation advisor, standing over my shoulder and cautioning, "Read the charters, Carolyn. Don't listen to what the bishop says. Read what he does." My supervising committee wanted theory, historiography, background, economic developments, architectural descriptions—everything except his personality. I finally bowed to their demands, of course, or I wouldn't have gotten my degree. But inside was that little voice that said, "Just you wait! One day I'll tell the REAL stories."

I continued the scholarly (read: stodgy) writing for fifteen years, always wanting to be more of a story-teller than the academic world would allow. The classroom was my only outlet, and I admit to telling some favorite scandalous stories to some of my upper-division classes. But retirement held out the real promise that I could finally let my imagination run free. I could write what I wanted to write.

So here I am, many years into my retirement and embarked on a new career as a novelist. Enter Perversity, stage left. What am I doing with my writing time? I'm deep into scholarly research. I'm still studying people, and the sources of my information are, for the most part, their letters, diaries, and journals. But now it's my inner voice that keeps warning, "Read the newspapers, the military dispatches, and the Congressional Record, Carolyn. Don't listen to what the gentleman says. Read what he does."

Could I tell a good, rousing story with no more information than whatever the letter collections provided? Certainly. But would I be satisfied with the result? Probably not. The curse (or blessing) of an author with a historical background is the need to get the facts straight first. Then the story can almost tell itself. More important, that nagging voice is making a promise to a future reading audience: "You can trust what you read here. I've done my research."

Mapping Your Way through Time and Space

Writers of fantasy and science fiction have one enormous advantage over the rest of us. They write about worlds that exist only in their imaginations, which means that none of their readers will show up at a book talk or in a review to point out errors. The rest of us must expect residents to challenge our statements whenever we write about their home towns.

My South Carolina readers are unusually possessive about their cities and their history. I once mentioned a church, only to be challenged by a Charleston tour guide who pointed out that no such building existed where I had placed it on Logan Street. I was able to respond with the detail that the church I mentioned had burned to the ground in the great Charleston fire of 1861; the congregation did not rebuild it. Other readers have pointed out streets whose names have changed and buildings about whose locations I have been slightly off. I don't mind such questions, but they keep reminding me that I need to know the places I describe. I keep references handy when I'm writing so that I can look up a street location, or the date of construction for new buildings. I'm careful to check varieties of plants and wildlife. And for my Civil War books, I consult records of which South Carolina military units participated in which battles, who their leaders were, and how many casualties they suffered.

I've also learned that any effort I make to figure out the details of chronology at the beginning of a writing project saves me many hours of rewriting later. In historical fiction, timing is vital. Without a thorough command of historical events, a seat-of-the-pants author runs the risk of including characters with anachronistic opinions, misdating known facts, or (horrors of horrors!) having a long-dead character suddenly reappear later in the book. I use timelines to avoid such problems.

In my Civil War stories, such details became increasingly important when I realized how many sources of information I had, and how great was the potential for them to contradict each other. I rely on a chronology of the Civil War itself. I double-check government documents, which frequently bear incorrect dates. I have, for example, a massive historical work that recounts the activities of the Port Royal Experiment, well-documented but not always well-dated. Footnotes referring to actions tend to record when the official wrote the report, not when the event occurred. I use a great many personal letters and diaries, each of which has a slightly different slant and the possibility that relatives censored the materials.

Because the potential for disaster is enormous, I devote much of my writing time to research. On the bright side, of course, is the fact that Charleston, South Carolina, is a top-rated tourist destination, so I'm always happy to use research as an excuse to visit. New writers might want to choose appealing locations for their stories so that they can chalk up some vacation time as a work-related expense.

What a Difference a Date Makes

While working my way through four different versions of Laura Towne's diary, I made a small, but amazingly significant, discovery. I was leafing through a handwritten copy, looking for a particular comment, when a date discrepancy caught my eye. One entry was dated July 19, 1862. The next one was July 20, 1901. Then came July 21, 1901 and then July 22, 1862.

Obviously, the person making the copy wrote down the current year instead of 1862. I've made the same mistake myself. When you are writing dates, it is all too easy to write down the current year instead of the appropriate one. History students do it on exams all the time, and their professors get a chuckle out of reading that Attila the Hun died in 1998. We've all misdated checks, particularly at the beginning of a new year. I've seen a Jeopardy contestant or two make the same mistake—one that cost them hundreds of dollars.

Now a history student may not know the right answer. And a Jeopardy contestant may be guessing. But this is not the same sort of mistake. When you list the wrong date for something you know very well, it almost always is a date that has some other significance. In this case, I think it is pretty conclusive evidence that someone copied the diary in 1901. That makes this version the earliest of the four extant copies, and the only one of the four known to the two people who were most involved with it—Laura and Ellen.

But 1901 is even more significant! That's the year that Laura died—on February 20, if I remember correctly. Here's what I think happened. When the twentieth century approached, Laura Towne was seventy-five years old. She was undoubtedly already ill, and, because of her extensive medical training, I am equally sure that she knew she was suffering from a potentially fatal illness. She would have begun putting her affairs in order, and one of the things she wanted to do was make a copy of the diary for her dear friend, Ellen Murray.

She shortened some of the entries and omitted others. She corrected her intemperate judgments as she went along. She was, in fact, composing her obituary—writing out the story of her life as she wanted it to be known. And she was probably not able to finish the task. The handwritten copy stops with the events of May 28, 1864. The original diary might have continued much longer.

Does this incorrect date prove that Laura wrote the copy? No, probably not. Ellen could have made the copy in the months after Laura died. But it increases the probability that the handwriting is indeed Laura's.

Don't Believe Everything You Read

Write this rule on a rock: "Always check the identity of your source." The more information becomes instantly available over the internet, the more careful you have to be. There's a wealth of material out there; there is also a never-ending supply of quacks, polemicists, and other angry people. Don't accept anything without finding some substantial supporting evidence.

Let's start by calling attention to a particularly dangerous area —personal letters or diaries that have been transcribed, copied, or edited by someone else. The Italian language has an important proverb: *Traduttore traditore*. It means, roughly, "a translator is a traitor." Spanish provides a similar thought: *E que traduce, traiciona*, or "He who translates is guilty of a betrayal." I kept the Italian version posted on the wall right above my office computer while I was working on a translation of Latin letters, just to remind myself that my English translation should reflect nothing but what the author wrote, not what I thought he should have written.

Back when I was first starting to research *A Scratch with the Rebels*, I traveled to Penn State University to sift through an enormous collection of materials from my great-uncle's 100th Pennsylvania Regiment. Seven large boxes in the library basement held a conglomeration of original letters, newspaper clippings, and typescript copies of other letters and diaries from members of the regiment. It appeared that no one had made an effort to preserve the materials because the original documents were often faded and ripped. I was grateful for the typescripts and spent much of my limited time reading those because they took less time and effort. The collection as a whole was so valuable for what I was doing that I didn't worry much about authenticity. Other descendants of the Roundheads had, after all, collected it, and a college English professor who taught in the county where the regiment originated had compiled the collection.

A bit later, I was at the public library in New Castle, Pennsylvania, this time looking for newspaper articles that would reveal how much the people back home knew of the war and how they felt about it. At one point, the librarian came into the archives to chat. She casually mentioned an elderly gentleman who had been there several years earlier. He had been looking for evidence that the regimental commander had been having an affair with the nurse who traveled with them. He had insisted that the chaplain had been quite upset about their relationship. Had I seen anything about that, she asked. I dismissed it out of hand. After all, I had just finished reading a typescript of Reverend Browne's letters, and I had not seen a single mention of such a thing. I dismissed it as utter nonsense. The librarian was relieved; Col. Leasure was a New Castle native and a local hero. She wanted nothing to sully his name.

I, too, put it out of my head for the moment, but I became intrigued by the possibility. Col. Leasure was a dapper little fellow. Nurse Nellie was young and very attractive. And Reverend Browne was a straight-laced Calvinist. When I went to the Military History Institute in Carlyle to investigate their holdings, I was pleased to learn that they possessed the original letters from Reverend Browne—some three hundred of them. I asked for the collection and put my husband to work on one stack while I plowed through the other. "Look for any mention of Nellie," I told him.

It didn't take long! These original letters were full of innuendo, snarling attacks on Nellie's character, and semi-veiled accusations of improper relationships. It was clear that the straight-laced chaplain had hated the nurse with a finely-honed passion and that he resented the fact that the colonel seemed to favor her. But why the difference between these letters and the transcript? When I asked the archivist, he shrugged and said, "Well, Browne's granddaughter was the one who prepared the typescript before we received the letters."

And there was the answer to at least part of the puzzle. The granddaughter had the opportunity to sanitize the collection, systematically removing anything that might have reflected poorly on her beloved ancestor. It didn't prove, of course, whether or not there had been an affair. It only explained why I had not reached the same conclusion as the elderly gentleman who believed that Browne was right.

I remain grateful for the discovery. It gave rise to my next book, *Beyond All Price*, and in that novel, I dealt with the question of the affair. I won't give away my conclusion, but I can tell you that I would have written a much different book if I had not read the original letters for myself.

But Sometimes There Are No Answers

One of the first—and hardest—lessons I have had to learn about research is that sometimes you just can't find the answers. In a few instances, that may be a good thing, of course, since there may be good reasons that someone wants to hide the facts. When you need information, however, missing details can be maddening. It's important to know when to stop hunting.

In 1992, I was working on a translated edition of Latin letters written by a twelfth-century Anglo-Norman bishop. One letter, in particular, was causing me problems as I tried to identify a person referred to only by his name, Milo. Medieval scribes, you see, frequently abbreviated words to save precious vellum, and their abbreviations can be confusing to later readers. In this case, there was a single word with two possible meanings. The word that came before Milo's name had a mark at the end that might—or might not —have been a sign of an abbreviation. If that is what it was, then Milo was a messenger or someone who was delivering the letter in question. If it was NOT an intentional abbreviation mark, the sentence identified Milo as the scribe who had written the letter. Other scholars had disagreed on which was the correct reading.

Foolishly, I thought I could solve the mystery. The earliest copy of the letter appeared in a manuscript held by one of the colleges in Oxford. Since I happened to be teaching in a summer program at that college, I assumed it would be an easy matter to get a close-up look at that word. I wanted to decide for myself whether it was an intentional mark or something accidental, such as a spatter from a broken quill or even a fly speck on the page.

I presented myself at the library soon after arriving in England and found the door barred by the She-Who-Must-Be-Obeyed librarian. "No," she said. "You may not come in." Well, she outweighed me by at least one hundred pounds, and when I say she blocked the door, she physically did so. Our little summer program, she told me, was only renting space at the college. I had no academic credentials in England; her library was only for real scholars or researchers. No amount of pleading by the head of our program would budge her. And that was the end of that.

I was not ready to give up. Milo's identity still puzzled me. So four years later, I went back, this time carrying official letters from my college and my PhD-granting university. It didn't matter. I still could not gain entrance. The librarian agreed, finally, to send me a microfilm copy of the manuscript, and a year later it arrived. Problem solved? Nope! You can't identify ink marks from a photo.

Fast forward to 2002. A third trip was in the works, and this time I contacted an English scholar who had been hired by that library to catalog their collection. He graciously interceded for me, and this time, after almost nine years of effort, I received permission to see the original manuscript. My official approval letter ordered me to report to the front door, credentials in hand, on a particular day and at a rather odd hour and precise minute. She-Who-Must-Be-Obeyed met me at the door and stood back to allow me to squeeze past her. She checked carefully to be sure I wasn't carrying a camera or a pen or pencil. Then she handed me a pair of sturdy white gloves and insisted that I put them on before I entered the reading room. She led me to a desk, where the manuscript lay on a cushion and announced that I had only fifteen minutes to examine it. The entire time, she stood looming over my right shoulder to be sure I did not damage the pages in any way.

There it was, finally—my mystery mark—and I still could not tell for sure. The ink colors were, perhaps, a bit off, which would suggest a later addition, but I could not be certain, and there was no way to magnify it or improve the lighting. If it was a fly speck, as I suspected, I could have discovered that with a simple flick of a fingernail, but the thick gloves and the looming supervisor made touching it impossible.

My fifteen minutes passed. I watched the elusive folio disappear from its cushion as the librarian ushered me out the door. There is no happy ending here. Some things you just can't find out, no matter how good your research skills. As a poker player might say, "You have to know when to fold 'em!"

Genealogical Road-Blocks: What's in a Name?

It couldn't be easier, right? The first time you visit an online genealogy site, they ask you to enter just the first and last name of the person in whom you are interested. Then they suggest you add as many other details as you happen to know. When I was starting the research for *Beyond All Price*, I entered a name (Nellie Chase), her birth state (Maine), and a year range of her birth (1835-1845). And I got results. One hundred and forty-seven of them, in fact! Who would have guessed that there would be that many Nellie Chases in the world, let alone in a single state? The site suggested I could narrow my results by entering more information, but more information was what I needed. I didn't know her parentage, her city, her death date, her husband's name, or any of the other things they suggested.

Did I eventually find my Nellie? Yes, I think so. But it took years, and that will have to be a separate story. If you are hunting for a family member, you may have more facts than I did at the beginning, but you are likely to run into many of the same problems. Here are some of the pitfalls that you need to avoid.

Census records look valuable, and they can be, but their worth depends entirely upon the competence of the person doing the recording. I just examined a record for my mother's family from the 1900 Pennsylvania Census. It listed the birth dates of two of her sisters as November 1877 and February 1878. Three months apart? Probably not!

For any record before the days of typewriters and computers, handwriting causes major problems. Some examples are marvelously clear; others are scrawls or overwritten so that it is impossible to decipher them. Then there are problems caused by mispronunciations or bad hearing or faulty transcriptions. The online version of the 1910 census shows my mother (Margaret McCaskey) as Marguett Mccacbey.

Nicknames cause their own set of difficulties. Nellie Chase always used the name Nellie, but her given name could have been Nell, Helen, Eleanor, or Ellen.

Family names change over time. A primary culprit may be the immigration record, on which an English approximation appears instead of an ethnic name. One branch of my father's family bore the surname of Arendt in Germany. They arrived in America as Aurand. Their friends the Muellers became the Millers.

Sometimes name differences are the result of a deliberate choice. I grew up knowing two cousins who had the same surname but with different pronunciations. Their fathers had a falling out and did not speak to each other, so one pronounced the last syllable of the family name as KO, while the other used KAWK. Both, however, spelled the surname as "-cock."

And then there's my husband's family. People frequently tell us that his last name should be "Schreiber." Well, it originally was. The family story says that John Schreiber, who fought in the Civil War, found that his discharge papers had spelled his name wrong.

He had two choices. He could refuse the paperwork and stay in the army. Or he could change his name to Schriber, take the discharge as written, and go home that very day. He accepted the name change! And his descendants have been Schribers ever since.

Don't misunderstand me. Genealogical research is great fun, and you can learn amazing things about your own family, including where someone buried the skeletons. But you do have to enter the search with a healthy dose of skepticism. The best family record sites offer you an option to search for an exact spelling or a rough one. I usually start with the exact search, but when that fails, a "sounds like" option is frequently the answer. After all, Nellie might have been Nelie, or Nelly, or Ellie, or even Ellen, as she turned out to be.

Online databases may help your search. Remember, however, that they don't come with guarantees that they are complete or that their information is accurate. I also recommend that you take full advantage of offers to use such sites without charge for a short period before committing to a yearly membership. You may find the site useful, of course, but it may contain nothing at all to help you.

- The Social Security Death Index has birth and death dates for deceased individuals with Social Security numbers who died after 1962 (after computerized records) through the current year.
- RootsWeb's WorldConnect Project is a database containing family files submitted by both amateur and professional researchers. For that reason, you can expect to find a large number of errors.
- FamilySearch, The Ancestral File and International Genealogical Index (IGI), a service provided by The Church of Jesus Christ of Latter-day Saints, contains information on millions of people worldwide, but these records too can be in error because many contributors are amateurs.

- The Ellis Island Database contains images of ship manifests documenting over 22 million people who entered the United States between 1892 and 1924 through Ellis Island and the Port of New York.
- The USGenWeb Project directory provides links to state and county genealogical resources.
- Ancestry.com may be the most useful for the beginning researcher. It offers ongoing help, access to millions of handwritten records, and the chance to connect with others who may be researching the same people. You must still be aware, however, that its information is only as good as the amateur investigators who compiled it. And some of them were making wild guesses or grasping at straws.

Evidence from Grandma's Attic

Another rule to write on a rock: "Don't go rooting around in Grandma's attic until you know enough about what you might find to recognize it when it falls into your lap."

My encounter with the treasures my grandmother preserved was a horrible disaster, although I did not realize it at the time. I was about nineteen or twenty, home from college for the summer and bored silly. My mother happened to mention that she needed to clean out the attic, and I thought I'd take a look around before she did so.

In a trunk of things she had kept after my grandmother died, I found some fabulous old clothes, a beaded evening bag worthy of a Charleston flapper, a couple of Kewpie dolls, and a mysterious white box tied with string. Inside the box, carefully protected from the rest of the objects in the trunk, were items for which I could see no apparent value. (Remember, I was young, stupid, and not yet a history buff.) Three yellow and crumbling newspapers lay on top.

All were from Beaver, Pennsylvania—one dated November 23, 1827; one dated December 15, 1841; another dated January 21, 1846. None seemed to contain anything other than local news, and I didn't spot any familiar names, although each had a handwritten name at the top.

Among the other unexplainable objects were an obituary, a red ribbon tied to a blackened award of some sort with no discernible legend, a piece of tattered and unraveling gold fringe, a newspaper clipping about a World War I soldier in France, and a single daguerreotype of a Civil War soldier. All the other items in the box were letters from people whose names I did not recognize. Each had its envelope, although the stamps of each had been cut out.

"Odd," I thought, shaking my head at the foibles of old folks who saved such trivial items. I carelessly dropped the whole lot back into the trunk and went downstairs.

"Nothing important that I might want," I reported.

Now we fast-forward some twenty years. After my mother's death, I was left to clean out her house. Many of the items I had seen in the attic had disappeared by then, but I did find the little white box and stuffed it into the parcel of photos I was keeping. The award, the piece of fringe, and the daguerreotype were not in the box. By then I was a history graduate student, and I began to sift Grandma's treasures with a more educated eye.

I was most excited about a bundle of eight letters, all written during the Civil War. I had been looking for a research project for my American history seminar, and they seemed to hold great promise. And so they did. It took years of reading and researching, but they eventually provided the structure for my book, *A Scratch with the Rebels*, which tells the story of my great-uncle, Sergeant James McCaskey, a Union soldier who longed to see military action and died during his first battle. You can read a description of the book elsewhere on my website.

But what about the rest of the items in Grandma's attic? Well, a few of them helped me with some genealogical research in building

Grandma's family tree. I still have not figured out the importance of the newspapers, and their condition continues to deteriorate. There were a few other items that I did not even remember from my first exploration—a poem, the front of a greeting card, a couple of pages from a child's book. But most of all, I regret the loss of the items I did not recognize earlier and preserve.

These are the keepsakes that fell into my lap and then slipped through my fingers into oblivion because I did not know what I was seeing. The award? I think it may have been a medal from World War I that belonged to my mother's cousin, the subject of the newspaper clipping. The fringe? It was probably, although I cannot say for certain, a remnant of one of the battle flags of the 100th Pennsylvania Volunteer Regiment. And the daguerreotype was almost certainly the only photograph ever taken of James McCaskey in his Civil War uniform.

History doesn't come to you neatly packed and labeled with its level of importance. It may be dirty, wrinkled, or crumbling from age.

Don't Believe Everything You Read

Unfortunately, newspaper articles are as likely to be misleading as any other source. Consider this example, which turned up while my favorite researcher was looking for information about the 100th Pennsylvania (Roundheads) Regiment:

> *Altoona Times* (Altoona, PA) March 4, 1864
>
> In the early part of the present month, a soldier belonging to the 100th regiment, having re-enlisted for the war, obtained a thirty days' furlough and returned to his home in Lawrence county, about four miles from Darlington, and almost adjoining the Beaver county line. The man was married, and during his absence, his wife contracted an acquaintance with a scamp in the

neighborhood, which culminated in a criminal intimacy between the parties. Of all this, however, the husband was in complete ignorance, and upon his return home he took up his abode with his wife, unconscious of her infidelity or of the plot which was even then maturing against his life.

It appears that soon after his arrival it was agreed between the woman and her paramour that he should be put out of the way, and one night, while the unsuspecting man lay asleep in his bed, the guilty pair approached him, and slipping a noose, which they had previously prepared, over his head, they threw the other end over a beam which extended across the dwelling, and pulling on it with all their might, they swung the wretched man off the bed, and in a moment almost had him in such a position that resistance on his part became impossible. They had their victim now completely in their power; and the deliberation which marked their after movements shows a degree of cold-bloodedness unequalled almost in the annals of crime.

Finding that death did not take place as soon as they had expected, they fastened the rope, which up to this time they had held over the beam, the body of their victim writhing in his death agony from the other end, to a peg in the wall, and leaving the miserable man to his fate passed out of the house. After remaining outside long enough for strangulation to take place, they again entered the house, and taking down the now lifeless remains of the murdered man carried them to a coal bank in the vicinity, inside which they concealed them.

The next day it was noticed that the woman's paramour was rather flush of funds, and this, coupled with the fact that the soldier was missing, induced those who knew the guilty relations existing between the woman and the man to suspect that all was not right; so an inquiry was instituted through which the entire tragedy was brought to light.—The woman, struck with fear or remorse, made a confession of the whole affair, implicating her paramour as the principal in the murder, and both he and she were arrested and committed to jail at New Castle to await their trial for murder.

The gentleman from whom we obtain our report of the tragedy could not give us the names of the parties, but he vouches for the correctness of the facts as we have given them It is the most horrible affair, and naturally created great excitement in the community where it occurred.

Both David and I were fascinated. What a great story! Note how many specific details here give further reason to believe the whole tale. We were already combing the regimental rosters to find the soldier who disappeared in early 1864 when the following article turned up:

Evening Telegraph, Harrisburg, PA, March 12, 1864.
A SENSATION STORY SPOILED.—The New Castle Courant spoils the sensation story which has been going the rounds of the press for some days relative to the murder of a soldier at Enon Valley by his wife and paramour. The man did return as stated and discovered the infidelity of his wife, but left the neighborhood, either the same night or early the next morning, and though diligent inquiry was made, was not heard from until Wednesday last, when he turned up, alive and well, at Enon Valley, from whence he went to visit his father in Ohio.

His sudden disappearance excited fears in the minds of the neighbors, which were strengthened by the fact that his wife and her paramour had his watch and plenty of greenbacks. All the twaddle about the tight rope performance, and the parties or either of them having acknowledged their guilt or been arrested, was hatched in the excited imagination of a Pittsburg paper's informant. The guilty pair have left for parts unknown.

Thus perished a great plot for a novel. Sigh!

Where Did They Put Grandpa?

I have learned a lot about cemetery research from a mysterious headstone that bears the name of my great-uncle James McCaskey, who died in the Civil War. After much searching, I found his marker in the same Pennsylvania cemetery where many of my other McCaskey ancestors rest. It reads: "James McCaskey; Born April 12, 1839; Died June 16, 1862; James Island, S.C."

Those details are all correct; the military action on James Island was the Battle of Secessionville. The problem is that the notification of his death says that they never found his body. The official records say that the Confederate troops buried the Union soldiers killed in the battle (some 509 of them) in unmarked graves on the battlefield. North Sewickley Cemetery records indicated that in 1875, Mrs. Jane McCaskey purchased three adjoining plots and ordered three matching stones—one for her recently deceased husband John, one for herself, and one for her missing eldest son, James.

Sure enough, the marker next to the one for James marks the grave of my great-grandmother Jane McCaskey. But on the far side of her grave, the ground has given away, and a gravel road lies several feet below the resulting ledge. So where is Great-Grandpa John? There is no sign of him or his tombstone at all. Was he ever there? Did an earthmover carry him away when they built the road? Or is he in the plot marked with his son's tombstone? At this point, the solution to the problem becomes too macabre to consider, so I am willing to accept what I think I know without further investigation.

Lesson Number One: A tombstone does not always equal a real burial. James's headstone marks an empty grave, a not uncommon phenomenon during a war that swallowed up so many young men on distant battlefields. The Grand Army of the Republic honors James McCaskey's service every Memorial Day by placing a flag at the grave site, but even their records stop short of stating that he lies buried there.

Lesson Number Two: The lack of a headstone does not necessarily mean that no grave ever existed. As time passes, stones crumble, weeds take over, land erodes, and new demands for grave sites force owners to change the layout of their cemetery plots. Jane McCaskey's marker now teeters dangerously close to the edge of the cut-away bank. In fact, it leans on the roots of the tree just behind the stone. John's grave would have been on the far side since wives were nearly always buried to the left of their husbands. John has disappeared, but we know from court records and other documents that he lay in that location in 1875.

Lesson Number Three: Burial practices change over time. While I was planning this blog post, I received a message from another genealogist, a distant cousin of my husband's, who had found the graves of my husband's grandfather and great-grandfather. I was astonished to learn that both men were buried in the same plot at St. Mary Cemetery in Cleveland, Ohio—one above the other. The cemetery records show John Christoph Schreiber (1845-1889) in section A, lot 48 North grave 4 E.D. (which stands for extra depth, or at about eight feet). His son, John C. Schriber, Jr. (1867-1928) is in section A, lot 48 North, grave 4 O.T.(on top, or at about 4 feet).

Cemeteries can tell us a great deal about those whose lives we are researching. Sometimes, perhaps, they show us more than we wanted to know!

Cemetery Research Methods

Cemeteries can prove to be a rich source for genealogical research. Here are some suggestions for doing your cemetery explorations.

Gather as much information as you can before you visit the

cemetery, unless, of course, you're just curious and not looking for anything or anyone in particular. Assuming you are interested in specific individuals, start by asking questions. If you know the cemetery you plan to visit, check with the caretaker or sexton to see if there is a directory. If the cemetery is no longer an active one, look for the pastor of the nearest church. Or try the local history section of the public library.

An obituary from a local newspaper can tell you which cemetery to visit. That's how David Welch and I eventually found the grave of Nellie M. Chase. Her obituary, reprinted in a Reading, Pennsylvania, newspaper, said she was living in Paris, Tennessee, at the time of her death, where she and her husband ran the railroad hotel. It also made it clear that she died in Louisville, Kentucky. That information led to a local newspaper article about yellow fever deaths in Paris, Tennessee, and a reference to a book on her employer, the L & R Railroad, which in turn gave the name of the cemetery in which the railroad company had buried her and her husband. After that, it only took a quick inquiry to the Cave Hill Cemetery in Louisville to discover the exact location of their burial plots and to get a photograph of their headstones.

Take the right equipment with you. Plan to take notes on every headstone you identify, but also be sure to have a camera. Notes have a way of perpetuating small errors. You'll want a picture later to double-check the details. Don't forget the insect spray. Mosquitoes can be formidable guards against your investigations. And unless the cemetery has an excellent landscaper, take gardening gloves and pruning shears. I wanted to try to straighten Uncle James's headstone, but a crop of fresh poison ivy dissuaded me. A spray bottle of water also comes in handy. Inscriptions are easier to read when they are wet, and you may need to wash away soil accumulations.

Finally, be alert to the clues on the stones themselves. Carvings on the headstone may provide clues to religion or military service. Traditionally, Christian graves face the east; i.e., the headstone is at the west end of the plot and the foot of the coffin at the east end, in preparation for Resurrection Day. For that reason, inscriptions on a headstone will be clearer if you take the picture in the morning. Tombstones frequently bear birth and death dates, although birth years are less to be trusted than death years. An inscription reading "Beloved Wife" usually means the woman's husband was still alive at her death. Unmarried sons and daughters are more likely to be buried near their parents. The graves of a wife or a couple near small unmarked stones may indicate the deaths of unnamed infants. Death dates can tie a victim to a natural disaster such as an earthquake or an epidemic of influenza or yellow fever. But as always, a researcher must accept any such evidence with a high degree of skepticism until there is confirmation from another source.

WRITING AND REWRITING
"The Best Laid Plans o' Mice and Men"

Robert Burns' "To a Mouse" is a sad ode to a rodent who suffers a terrible accident. The subtitle, "On Turning Up Her Nest with the Plough," tells the whole story. The "wee, sleetet, cowran, tim'rous beaste" has done nothing to deserve her fate, just as the farmer had no intention of disrupting her little home. Yet all is lost, and all the poet can offer is an observation that the well-intentioned plans of mice and men often go astray, leaving nothing behind but grief and fear. There's not much comfort there for a writer who discovers that her storyline has wandered away from its intended goal or that the writing is so bad as to be unreadable.

It may be too late for the poor little mouse to rebuild her cozy shelter before winter sets in, but, fortunately for you as a writer, all is not lost. Never fear, poor timorous writer. You can keep making corrections and improvements for as long as necessary. That is, in fact, one of the benefits of being a self-publishing author. You don't have a publisher who is establishing impossible deadlines or a sneering editor to tell you you've written nothing but drivel. Remember that we call what you have just written the "first draft." Now is not the time to despair but to welcome several rounds of writing and rewriting.

Difficulties with Your Story Line

When you face multiple problems, the best approach is to deal with the biggest ones first, so that whatever follows does not loom as quite so large. Do you remember my first experience with a NaNoWriMo project? I finished my 50,000 words and promptly sent the manuscript off to CreateSpace to have it turned into a real printed book. I'm not sure what kind of magic I thought might occur during that print process. But when the finished book came back to me I was horrified at how bad it was. The problem, of course, was the very idea that the first draft of a story written at breakneck speed might ever be worthy of being called a book at all. In the following years, I noted, the NaNoWriMo managers dropped that promise of a printed book. Rightly so.

We'll assume that you have taken all the bits and pieces assembled during the research phase and arranged them into some order as a first draft. Put it away. Take a vacation. Start a house remodeling. Take cooking classes. Do anything except writing for at least a month—maybe more. By the time you come back to the manuscript, you will have forgotten much of what you were proud of at the time you wrote it. Now is the time to look at that draft with a harsh and unforgiving eye. On that theory, let's start with your story arc. Answering a series of questions will put you back on the right writing track.

Once more, who is your leading character and what is his or her primary goal? What stands in the way of achieving that goal? The answers must be readily apparent to you and your readers. Without those bits of story structure, you don't have a book.

How's your timing? Does something happen within the first few pages to catch the reader's attention and make her want to learn more? Too much backstory or description, however, will cause terminal boredom.

Does the suspense build from beginning to end? If you give away the solution too early, the reader will leave the book unfinished. And did you stop writing when the final problem was solved?

Now, look at each of the mounting problems that confront your hero. At each level, is there a logical and believable solution? In some early Roman dramas, the answer came when an Olympic god dropped onto the stage from above. The literary device is called a *deus ex machina*—a god delivered by a mechanical device. No swooping miracles allowed today unless you are George Martin writing *Game of Thrones*.

Have you left any dead ends or unanswered questions? Does one of your characters disappear because you forgot about him? Did you set up an unsolvable problem and then abandon it? You have only two choices. Solve the problems or get rid of them entirely.

Have you made any silly mistakes? Did your character start out fearing snakes and then later turn up with a pet boa constrictor? Did someone die and then reappear in a later chapter? Did Aunt Molly change her name to Aunt Mabel? Does one of your characters acquire a new relative without explanation? Do your dated events make sense? Catch those errors before your readers do.

The Problem of Voice

Most of us recognize good writing when we see it, but we don't often interrupt our sheer delight in a passage to analyze it. We don't ask what it was that made that particular group of words stand out. We move on, anxious to read more of "the good stuff." When the writing is bad, our responses are more varied. Sometimes we just nod off over a book or article because it is not interesting enough to keep our minds alert. Other times, we put the book down and forget we were trying to read it. When the writing is terrible, teachers shake their heads in despair and slap a C- on the paper. And once again, we move on in search of something better, without taking the time to figure out exactly what it was that elicited our sighs.

The process of writing is so complicated—and so different for each writer—that I've been struggling with how to describe the difference between good and bad writing. One morning, help arrived in the shape of an email from a colleague who was deep into grading at the moment. She passed along a couple of examples that summed up the distinction:

"This sentence has five words. Here are five more words. Five-word sentences are fine. But several together become monotonous. Listen to what is happening. The writing is getting boring. The sound of it drones. It's like a stuck record. The ear demands some variety.

"Now listen. I vary the sentence length, and I create music.

Music. The writing sings. It has a pleasant rhythm, a lilt, a harmony. I use short sentences. And I use sentences of medium length. And sometimes, when I am certain the reader is engaged, I will offer him a sentence of considerable length, a sentence that burns with energy and builds with all the impetus of a crescendo, the roll of the drums, the crash of the cymbals—sounds that say listen to this, it is important."

I want to write the idea on a rock: "The ear demands variety."

[Full credit for the paragraph goes first to Gary Provost, and then to Roy Peter Clark who quoted him in *Writing Tools*. And secondary credit goes to a blog post written several years ago by Rob McDougall.]

Don't Let Your Modifiers Dangle Out There

Life is unfair. Those who want to be comedians have a difficult time being funny. Those who are trying to write something serious often end up being unintentionally hilarious. Assuming that you do not want your readers to laugh at you instead of with you, here are some examples of how NOT to write. Consider the pictures painted by the following sentences:

- Having been thrown in the air, the dog caught the stick.
- Smashed flat by a passing truck, Rover sniffed at the remains of a half-eaten hamburger.
- The young girl was walking the dog in a short skirt.
- The dog was chasing the boy with the spiked collar.
- Piled up next to the washer, I began doing the laundry.

You'd never write something so silly, you say? Well, try these, all taken from student papers in a creative writing course.

- Standing on the balcony, the ocean view was magnificent.
- I heard that there was a revolution on the evening news.
- While taking out the trash, the sack broke.
- Having laid an egg weighing two pounds, the farmer proudly displayed his favorite ostrich before the photographers.
- Having given birth to six kittens, my girlfriend anxiously watched her exhausted cat, Mrs. Whiskers.
- Ugly, warty creatures with protruding noses and bat-like wings, architecture students find gargoyles endlessly fascinating as expressions of the grotesque.
- The robber was described as a six foot-tall man with brown hair and blue eyes and a mustache weighing 150 pounds.
- Deciding to pack up for college, my dog stared sadly at me as I bustled about the room.
- Having applied a tourniquet, the bleeding finally stopped.
- The policemen finally stopped the criminal using pepper spray and handcuffs.
- David struck down Goliath fighting against a giant.
- Famous throughout the world for his shocking makeup, wailing lyrics, and androgynous wardrobe, the editor of our church newspaper chose to interview Marilyn Manson.
- In awe, circling the coldest regions of outer space in an endless dance, the astronomers watched the planet, Pluto.

Each one of those sentences contained an example of a dangling modifier—an adjective, a prepositional phrase, or a participial phrase—placed too far away from the word it was supposed to modify. Fortunately, once you start to look for these, they tend to jump out and grab your attention. Even better, the solution is easy. First, check for any modifying words that appear at the beginning of a sentence. That's where we get into the most trouble, primarily because we're trying so hard to vary the sentence structure. When you find one of these, underline the closest noun that appears in the sentence, either before or after the modifier. That's the word the phrase is modifying, whether you want it to or not. Ask yourself if the modifier and the noun fit together logically. If they do, great! If they don't, you've detected a dangling modifier. Rewrite the sentence.

Passives and Other Problems

Every writer needs to pay attention to awkward wording, misused words, bland adjectives, misplaced commas, and boring verbs. But other problems are harder to spot. What else could be wrong? Let's try a different round of tweaking.

Eliminate all instances of passive voice. A sentence will usually be much stronger if the subject is the one performing the action. "I was spanked by my father" is whiny. "My father spanked me" is angry and accusatory.

How do you find passives? The various forms of the verb *to be* (am, is, are, was, were, being, been) do not necessarily make a sentence passive, but it is hard to imagine a passive sentence without one. Every time you find one of these words, ask yourself if the subject is acting or the recipient of the action. If the subject is not the actor, rewrite the sentence.

- The child was being beaten by a bully. (Passive—the subject is having something done to him.)
- The child was beating the drum. (Active—the subject did the action.)

Check your dialogue. Does it sound like real people talking? Try eavesdropping on real conversations while riding a bus or waiting in a checkout line. You'll see that people don't often use complete sentences, and speakers don't politely wait their turn. They jump in whenever they feel like it. Real people also do not use each other's names very often. When they do, it is usually significant. The speaker is angry or demanding attention.

Have you used too much description in identifying the speakers? Is it essential to identify the speaker? If your characters are strong, they will have distinctive speech patterns that will automatically identify them. You can usually get rid of "Tom said," before every pronouncement.

The only exception to that rule may be when you are handling a conversation in which more than three people are involved. And even in that circumstance, you probably don't want to use any tags beyond "said" or "asked" or "answered." Consider this example: "I don't want to leave," she sniffled. Now, she may have said that, and she may have been sniffling, too, but she can't sniffle (which involves breathing in) and speak (which involves breathing out) at the same time. If you are determined to keep every word, then punctuate it as two sentences: "I don't want to leave." She sniffled.

Don't be too descriptive. Let the speaker's words tell the reader how the words were said. Consider this horrible example: "Help!" she shouted helplessly. It conveys the same information four times in four words: the word itself; the exclamation point; the descriptive tag, "she shouted," and that ridiculous adverb at the end. "Help!" Each one tells the reader everything necessary.

Vary your sentence structure and length. Don't start every sentence by giving subject—verb—object. But don't start every sentence with a conjunction, either. I have to watch my habit of starting with an adverb or prepositional phrase. All grammatical sentences are acceptable. You just need variety to keep your reader awake.

Keep each page visually inviting. Try staring at the page from across the room. Do you have enough white space to make the page look attractive? Make sure you don't have long segments of narration. Perhaps you give more description than is needed. Does the page look like a solid block of print? You may need to break it into several shorter paragraphs or add some dialogue to interrupt the descriptions in the middle. Dialog helps to keep the pacing, to produce the music of the spoken word.

At the other extreme, you don't want a whole page full of dialog, especially if it is the rapid-fire kind in which each person speaks only one or two words. Such a conversation might work well in a staged play, but on a book page, it will look like a mistake. If the page has a narrow band of print at the left margin, and gaping areas of white space on the right, you'll need to break up the conversation with some descriptive paragraphs.

Also look for a river of white space running through the middle of your lines. You can't spot this flaw until the typesetter has finished, but sometimes the spaces between words line up, one above another, line after line, in such a way as to produce an eye-distracting white path through the text. The fix is easy. Change just a word or two and the river disappears.

Check your transitions. Chapters should wrap up some loose ends but leave enough questions unanswered to make your reader want to keep reading. A new chapter may switch point of view, or location, or jump from one period to another. But if such changes take place, be sure to make them clear at the start. The first words of a new chapter may need to be some variety of these:

- Meanwhile, back at the police station . . .
- The next day, Tom traveled to . . .
- After school, the children . . .
- When the plane landed in Paris, the inspector . . .

Problems of Weak Vocabulary

Look for words that are redundant or indefinite.

- BACK—She eased back into her chair, letting out a sigh that hissed exasperation. Better: She leaned into her chair.
- UP (when the direction is obvious)—He jumped up onto the porch. Better: He jumped onto the porch.
- DOWN (when the direction is obvious)—He looked down at his feet. Better: He looked at his feet.

Define indefinite words.

- Reconsider your use of IT, THEY, SOME, MANY, FEW
- Name the object. Who are they? Quantify some, many and few.
- If you mention an animal, don't refer to the creature as a cat, dog, horse. Give the particular breed, sex, or color.
- If you mention a car, give the make, model, and color.
- If you talk about time, define the duration—ten minutes or whatever.

Check for those words that frequently occur throughout the manuscript and substitute another similar word.

- WALKED—try strode, ambled, sauntered, strolled, shuffled, staggered.
- RAN—try jogged, scurried, scampered, hurried, dashed, rushed, loped.
- CRIED—whimpered, sobbed, sniveled, bawled, wailed, blubbered, howled.

Consider your adjectives. Are they boring? Why? Choose descriptive terms that will play on the senses and add sparkle to the text.

- COLD—How cold? Icy, bone-chilling, numbing, frosty, Arctic.
- HOT—How hot? Blistering, broiling, sizzling, scalding.

Tighten the manuscript further. Check for words such as FELT, FIGURED, and HEARD. Omit these words by explaining how the character felt and what he heard or saw. You don't need to say that a character looked at someone before speaking. That's assumed. However, if the character looked away, this might indicate the character's lack of receptiveness.

Search for these words: STARTED, BEGAN, KNEW, REALIZED, APPEARED. You don't need these words to introduce an action.

- She knew John lied. Better to say: John lied. The point of view tells us she knew.
- She started to cross the room. Better to say: She crossed the room
- She realized he hated her. Better to say: He hated her.

Avoid slang unless you are using it deliberately to help establish a character's identity. Nothing changes faster than slang, so don't date yourself or your book by using a word that may go out of fashion before your reader gets to read it.

Avoid specialized terms and abbreviations until you have defined them clearly for the reader.

Conquering Commas and Other Punctuation

Do rules about how to use commas make you turn purple? No wonder! Let's see if we can make them easier. Commas are a relatively recent invention. When the Romans first started writing things down, they didn't have punctuation marks. They didn't have any lower case letters or use spaces between words either, so:

ALLTHEIRWRITINGLOOKEDLIKETHISOBVIOUSLYTHATWASAPROBLEMFORTHEPOORREADER.

Just as a space shows a reader when a word stops, commas tell a reader when to breathe. They were helpful when sentences grew longer than "Me hungry. Kill deer." Try reading this sentence out loud: "At the grocery, we bought the following items: peas and carrots and macaroni and cheese and chicken and dumplings."

Obviously, you need to replace some of the conjunctions with commas, but which ones? That will depend on how many separate items appeared on the cash register tape. Did you buy peas, carrots, a box of dry macaroni, a package of cheese, a whole chicken, and some frozen dumplings for a total of six items? Or did you just buy three: peas and carrots, macaroni and cheese, and chicken and dumplings? Say the two versions aloud and listen for the differences.

Other comma rules apply to confusing grammatical structures like appositives, direct address, and restrictive versus nonrestrictive clauses. You won't need such esoteric terms if you use the pause rule. Consider this scenario. A fire occurred in the middle of the night at a rooming house where several men were living. Deaths resulted. How many died? Listen for the pauses. Add commas.

- The men who were asleep died in the fire. (The sleepers died while the poker-players did not.)
- The men, who were asleep, died in the fire. (They were all asleep and they all died.)

Academics sometimes argue over what is called the Oxford comma. That's the one that appears before the final *and* in a series. When I read a series of terms (like pens, note-books, pencils, and erasers), I hear a pause after pencils, so I always use the Oxford comma. In other words, I follow my own rule about hearing commas. You may, however, encounter an editor who argues the point with you. It's probably best to give in, because editors always win.

Write this on a rock: A natural pause indicates a comma.

When Do You Use a Hyphen? And Why?

Hyphens are much less common today than they used to be. In most instances, you can probably get away with omitting them entirely. Here are just a few exceptions.

Hyphens are used in many compound words to show that the component words have a combined meaning (e.g., a pick-me-up, mother-in-law, good-hearted) or that there is a relationship between the words that make up the compound: for example, rock-forming minerals are minerals that form rocks. But you don't need to use them in every type of compound word.

With compound adjectives formed from the adverb well and a participle (e.g., well-known), or from a phrase (e.g., up-to-date), you should use a hyphen when the compound comes before the noun:

- well-known brands of coffee
- an up-to-date account

but not when the same words come after the noun:

- His music was also well known in England
- Their figures are up to date.

It's important to use hyphens in compound adjectives describing ages and lengths of time: leaving them out can make the meaning ambiguous. For example, "250-year-old trees" refers to trees that are 250 years old, while "250 year old trees" could equally refer to 250 trees that are all one year old.

Use a hyphen to separate a prefix from a name or date, e.g., post-Aristotelian or pre-1900.

Use a hyphen to avoid confusion with another word: for example, to distinguish re-cover (provide something with a new cover) from recover (get well again).

Hyphens can also be used to divide words that are not usually hyphenated. They show where the break could come at the end of a line of writing. Always try to split the word in a sensible place, so that the first part does not mislead the reader: for example, hel-met, not he-lmet; dis-abled, not disa-bled.

Hyphens are also used to stand for a common second element in all except the last word in a list, e.g., You may see a yield that is two-, three-, or fourfold.

Link compound proper nouns and adjectives with a hyphen. For example, "Italian-American."

Use a hyphen with numbers and fractions. For example, "four-fifths," "thirty-eight" and so on.

We Can Do Without Semicolons

Once you've mastered the comma, most English grammar books ask you to consider the semicolon. Please don't. Semicolons are pretentious, and they serve no needed function, except in one instance. The rule says, when you have two independent clauses (two subjects, two verbs), you can join them with a conjunction or a semicolon. But only academics use them that way; if you're writing fiction or guidelines that you want to be useful, stick with connecting words (There, now. Didn't that sound stuffy?)

Only use a semicolon in one instance—in a series in which each item has a qualifying phrase attached loosely to it. Consider this sentence and its variation:

"I invited Eric, the boy in the blue shirt, Emily, a friend who plays the piano, Joshua, a neighbor from down the street, Sam, the kid nobody likes, and Sally." (How many people received an invitation? Nine or five?) If you leave all the commas in, as this sentence did, you mean you invited nine people, some of them with names and some with identifying tags.

"I invited Eric, the boy in the blue shirt; Emily, a friend who plays the piano; Joshua, a neighbor from down the street; Sam, the kid nobody likes; and Sally." The punctuation is correct here, but it, too, looks like an English teacher wrote it. (And remember, nobody loves an English teacher.)

When you are tempted to use a semi-colon, take a break from writing. Your readers will thank you for it.

Let's Abolish The Colon

If I could, I would abolish all colons from fiction or informal writing. Why? They fail to meet the primary definition of a punctuation mark. Hmmm? You've forgotten already, haven't you?

Punctuation marks were invented to help oral readers know when to breathe or when to stop talking, or when to raise the tone of the voice at the end of a question. The colon can not be pronounced, or breathed, or indicated by the tone of voice. The only thing it says is "A list is coming." And lists have no business cropping up in fiction. As a writer, you can be much more creative than that.

Now see what we've accomplished? We've eliminated the need for a whole key on the QWERTY keyboard. If I could, I would replace it with a much more useful one—your favorite expletive—for use every time you mistype a word or accidentally delete something important. (I once found a stick-on key with a four-letter word printed on it. It was non-functional but a great stress-reliever. Before I finished my first book, I had pounded the lettering right off it.)

Make Do with Fewer Exclamation Points

We can't do away with these entirely, but like the semicolon, I recommend that you use them as if they were as expensive as diamonds. One jewel, no matter how small, glitters and looks beautiful. Put a hundred of them in a pile, and they start looking like glass beads. The same thing is true of an exclamation point. If your character hits his thumb with a hammer, you can write down what he says in one of two ways:

"Ouch!"—or—"Ouch," he exclaimed. The punctuation mark is, of course, shorter and more efficient than the verb. But never do this: "Ouch!!!!!!!!!!!!!" Now you haven't shown pain or excitement. You've just built a picket fence, which will shut your reader off just as certainly as a real barrier.

Who Needs an Ampersand?

Do you even know what an ampersand is? Or where it originated? (Here's where my training in medieval history comes in handy.) An ampersand is that funny-looking symbol on the 7-key—&.

It originated in a medieval scriptorium, where overworked monks lettered Latin Bibles and charters by hand. Both to speed up their work and to save parchment, which was ridiculously expensive, they created symbols that worked like abbreviations. An ampersand is the Latin word *et* or *and*, written with a single swipe of the pen. It's the letter *e* with the tail crossed to form the *t*.

Unless you are a native speaker of Latin (in which case you are long-dead) or a monk (in which case you may be just hopelessly behind the times), you have no excuse for using it. I vote to send it to the same scrap heap as the colon, except for one example. Law firms, which tend to be old-fashioned and stuffy themselves, sometimes give themselves a name that they think looks impressive. Featherstone & Higgenbottom may have an important role to play in your novel. But writing "He bought fish & chips" looks silly and sounds worse. Remember, punctuation tells an oral reader what to do with his voice. Did you intend to say "He bought fish et chips"?

Spelling — Cna Ouy Rdea Htis?

Studies have demonstrated that most people look at the line above and have no trouble reading it as "Can you read this." Experts think that our minds are conditioned to switch the letters around until they form a recognizable word. That may be so, but fussy folks (like English teachers and other literary types) expect a writer to be able to spell. Nothing will get your manuscript tossed into the trash can more quickly than having misspelled words—especially if one of them happens to be the name of the agent or publisher you are trying to woo. I worry about today's teenagers who have grown up knowing how 2 txt w/ as few ltrs as psbl. We may have raised a whole generation of unemployable illiterates.

Grammar books will offer all sorts of spelling rules, some of which I know you've heard.

- I before E except after C. This one works sometimes, but it doesn't apply if the word contains an AY sound, (neighbor, vein), and there are other inexplicable exceptions (either, foreign).
- To add an ending to a word that ends with a silent E, drop the E before adding an ending that begins with a

vowel, (curve becomes curving), and keep the E if the ending begins with a consonant (true becomes truly). Of course, there are exceptions, such as mileage and judgment.
- When you add an ending to a word that ends with Y, change the Y to I and then add the ending (worry becomes worries). But the rule does not apply to adding -ING ((worrying) or when the Y follows a vowel (saying).
- Do you want to talk about doubling final consonants? I don't even want to try this one. The answer is you do, and you don't, depending on the number of syllables in the word and the placement of the accent. Don't ask. Look it up. That's one purpose of a dictionary.

Now, I wish I could offer you some easy rules, comparable to the comma rule, to get you past this problem. Surely phonics instructors and Sesame Street taught us how to pronounce our letters. But the English language, being typically English at times, does not lend itself to rules. Do you doubt that? Then think of these words and read this sentence out loud: Although all through the night, he had a rough cough, he thought it was because of the drought, and he didn't think he ought to spend the dough on a doctor. Tell me now, how do you pronounce the following letter combination: OUGH?

Here are the only rules I think you can trust.

- Use a spell-checker, but don't rely on it to catch every spelling error. It won't understand the difference between too, to, and two, for example, or any other pair of words that sound alike.
- Buy a good (new!) dictionary and check it whenever you are in doubt. Remember that the meanings of words change over time, old words become obsolete,

and new ideas and new technologies spawn whole fresh vocabularies.
- Don't try to be sophisticated by using English spelling for words like centre or colour. You sound as if you made a wrong turn somewhere in the middle of the Atlantic Ocean. (But if your publisher happens to reside in England, all bets are off.)

Look-Alikes and Sound-Alikes

When you are editing your manuscript, keep a sharp lookout for the following words. They differ by only one letter but have different uses and meanings.

ADVICE is a noun similar to recommendation. *I didn't ask for Samantha's advice, but she gave it to me anyway.*

ADVISE is a verb similar to recommend. *The doctor advised me to drink more water when I exercise.*

ALTAR is a raised structure in a church. *The congregation stood and faced the altar.*

ALTER means to change. *The book is great; don't alter a word of it.* (HAH!)

CAPITAL is a noun referring to a city or money, as well as an adjective that means most important or that precedes the word punishment. *Our capital goal is to raise the capital needed to fund the new project.*

CAPITOL is a government building. *Which architectural styles were popular when they built this capitol?*

CAVALRY is a horse-mounted military unit. *During the Civil War, cavalry units still ranked as elite troops.*

CALVARY is a hill mentioned in the Bible. *The crucifixion took place at Calvary.*

CITE is a verb meaning mention. *Be sure you cite at least five sources in your next research paper.*

SITE is a noun referring to location, whether physical or on the Internet. *There are mixed opinions about the best site for the new residence hall.*

COMPLEMENT is a noun or verb that means "adds to" or finishes. Note that "comple" begins both complement and complete. *Bethany always wears a scarf to complement her outfit.*

COMPLIMENT is a noun or verb similar to praise. *Although his stage persona is extroverted, Boswell gets embarrassed every time someone compliments his acting abilities.*

DESERT is a noun referring to a dry place or climate and a verb meaning leave. *I love water too much to live in a desert. Although Mary went to the party with Jon, she deserted him as soon as she found her other friends.*

DESSERT is a noun referring to a sweet food. The extra "s" in this word may come from the sugar. *My favorite dessert is warm chocolate cake with coconut ice cream.*

FARTHER is the preferred word when describing physical distance. *If I lived farther from campus, perhaps I would get more exercise.*

FURTHER generally refers to figurative distance or distance

in time. *Housing is an important topic; let's discuss it further tomorrow.*

ITS is the possessive form of the pronoun IT. *The cow jumped over its fence.*

IT'S is a contraction of IT IS. *It's time to build a higher fence.*

PRINCIPAL is an adjective meaning main or most important and a noun identifying a sum of money or the head of a school. Remember the saying, "The principal of your school is your pal"? *The principal reason we hired Mr. Jones as the new principal is that he is extremely creative.* [And I admit that sentence is too wordy!]

PRINCIPLE is a noun similar to rule or belief. *Maxine adhered to three basic principles when she wrote her novels: revise, revise, revise.*

STATIONARY is an adjective meaning not moving. *Although the scenery was dull, Jules enjoyed exercising on the stationary bicycle in his basement.*

STATIONERY is a noun referring to paper and other writing supplies. Notice the "er" in both stationery and paper. *Martha writes so many letters that she buys new stationery every month.*

A Few More Problematic Pairs

Here are some twins (and one triplet) that are a bit more complicated than the previous list.

ACCEPT is a verb that means agree with or receive. *We accept all major credit cards. I accept your explanation of these differences.*

EXCEPT is a preposition that means apart from something else. *Men are idiots. (Present company excepted.) I like all vegetables except turnips.*

ACUTE means sharp as in an angle, or describes a disease that rapidly develops and gets worse. *She developed acute appendicitis.*

CHRONIC illness or problem may also be severe, but it is long-lasting and lingering. *She has chronic hay fever.*

ADVERSE means unfavorable or hostile. *This summer we face adverse weather conditions.*

AVERSE means having an active feeling of repugnance or opposition. *He is not averse to buying a lottery ticket now and then.*

AFFECT is a verb that means to influence something. Remember, if something affects you, it has an effect on you. *The movie affected me so deeply that I cried all the way through it.*

EFFECT is a noun that means the result of something. (Just to complicate matters, these two words have specialized academic meanings, but for most of us, this distinction doesn't matter.) *Hot temperatures have an adverse effect on our ability to think clearly.*

CONTIGUOUS means touching or adjoining in space. *Alaska is not one of the forty-eight contiguous states because it does not share a border with any other state.*

CONTINUAL means repeated frequently. *His continual disruptions disturb those who attend our meetings.*

CONTINUOUS indicates something uninterrupted in time

or space. *The continuous murmur of the stream outside my window puts me to sleep.*

DISCREET means circumspect. *Members of Congress must be discreet about the information they learn as part of their duties.*

DISCRETE means having separate and distinct parts. *Our three branches of government should remain discrete, and discreet, too.*

DISINTERESTED describes having no bias or personal stake in an issue. *A disinterested person should settle the argument.*

UNINTERESTED means to have no interest in something. *I am uninterested in celebrity gossip.*

EMIGRATION is leaving a country. *His parents felt hurt by his emigration from the old country.*

IMMIGRATION is arriving into a new country. *The newly-settled west welcomed his immigration because he brought much needed skills with him.*

It all depends on where you stand in relation to the act. *As for the young man himself, he emigrated from Ireland and immigrated to Boston.*

FLOUT means to break a rule by flagrantly ignoring it. *He flouts traffic signs by speeding right through them.*

FLAUNT means to brag about something by showing it off. *He enjoys flaunting his fancy new car.*

PAST, the adjective, refers to something that has previously occurred. *Please forget about my past failures.*

PASSED, the verb, is the past tense of pass. *This time I passed my driver's test.*

Advanced Reading Copies (ARCs)

You need extra help before your book appears in print. No matter how carefully you have proofread your book—no matter how good your early editor may be—typos and other tiny errors can slip through without detection. You need fresh eyes to go over the manuscript before you say you have finished. Now, if you had a traditional publishing company, they would print off a few test copies (ARCs) and send them off to early readers, also known as beta readers. Since you're an indie author, you'll have to do that yourself. You probably can't afford to purchase a bunch of finished copies from your printer, but you can use your manuscript's .doc file in the same way. Most book lovers will not mind reading a new book on the computer screen. If someone asks you for the Kindle version, it's easy enough to find automatic file conversion services on the internet. Just recently I did a free .doc to .mobi conversion online so a beta reader could use it on her Kindle. The resulting file wasn't pretty, but it was close to being accurate. We identified just one word that the program misread.

Choose your beta readers carefully. Do not use your Aunt Mabel's next door neighbor or your pizza delivery person. They may be perfectly lovely individuals, but you need book experts, not just friendly folks who are curious about what you do. Nor do you need many people offering you advice. Shoot for quality, not quantity.

The very best beta readers are other writers. They love books. They probably read a lot for relaxation between writing sessions. This past spring while I was heavily engaged in writing my novel, I also read and reviewed nineteen books for a major book award program. In the process, I took a refreshing break from my struggles with plot and characterization. And at the same time, I learned a great deal about successful book structure and honed my ability to spot errors. In this business, as in any other, always give the necessary jobs to the busiest people. They are the ones who will get it done.

The first time I tried to use beta readers for one of my civil war novels, I made several mistakes. I sent out an open call and accepted every offer I received, even if I had never heard of the individual. A few were close friends who understood nothing about writing. From them, I received pleasant but unhelpful comments like, "I enjoyed the book," "Interesting," or "Good job." Others were casual internet friends who were quick to say, "Sure, I'll read your book," and then promptly forgot all about it. And then there was the woman who said, "Sorry, I just haven't had time to read it this year. Maybe after the holidays, I can get back to it." Another said, "It's a good story, but I think you should set it in the modern world and make the main character a Vietnam vet with PTSD."

Now I settle for two or three beta readers, each one of whom brings a particular qualification to the task. For my last book, I started with a fellow writer I met through a Camp NaNoWriMo challenge. We discovered that we both were working on books set in South Carolina at the beginning of the Civil War. Were we rivals? Of course not. Our stories were different, and we had varied perspectives. That meant we could learn from each other, and I jumped at the chance when she suggested that we do a beta-reader exchange. The second offer came from one of the other judges in the book contest I mentioned above. From watching her review the books we were both evaluating, I knew her to be fair, honest, and focused on details. The third was a faithful reader who has read every book I have written. She is also a writer whose historical knowledge I respect. Together the three beta readers provided useful comments that led me to do a quick polishing of the manuscript before it went to press.

The Final Word on Editing Your Book

Checking your work by using these guidelines will produce a more readable book. Will it then be perfect? Of course not. You still must be on the alert for omitted articles and prepositions. Look for spots where you may have done some cutting and pasting, leaving a few extra words behind. Other proof-reading tricks may help. Some people swear by reading the book backward, which may draw your attention to misspelled words. Enlist the help of willing friends, who may spot details your own eyes keep overlooking. Beta readers and fellow writers who are willing to exchange reading duties with you may be especially useful. Consider using one of the new software applications like Grammarly that checks these details for you. You'll get one final check if you publish on Kindle. Don't be surprised when they send your first submitted copy back, telling you to correct some spelling errors. Say thank you graciously, and change any real slip-ups. You didn't expect to be perfect, did you?

DESIGNING THE FINAL PRODUCT

"Ce fromage est délicieux."

A natole is a serious-minded and honorable French mouse in a children's book by Eve Titus. He wears a cocky beret, tootles around Paris on his tiny bicycle, and sports a bright red neck scarf. One day he heard people complaining about mice. All rodents, they said, were sneaky little thieves, always stealing their food rather than working for it. He was embarrassed and decided to do something to repair the reputations of his fellow mice. So he set out to find honest work that would be helpful to humans. At a cheese factory, he created a job for himself as a cheese taster. At night he would sample the cheeses and leave little notes about their quality, signing them only as Anatole. He had such a sophisticated palette that the cheese company flourished. The owners were grateful but could never identify their most important employee.

Self-publishers would be wise to follow Anatole's example. Although it is becoming more and more acceptable to be a self-publisher, a few poorly designed and formatted books have hurt the reputation of all independent publishers. I know. As a reviewer, I've seen some awful examples—tiny margins, missing page numbers, typos, grammatical errors, blurry pictures. If you are going to accept full responsibility for the appearance as well as the content of your book, you must be prepared to create error free copy and to follow all the traditional design rules of the major publishing houses.

The Good Old Days

Once upon a time (in honor of our mousey fairy tale theme), authors did not have to worry about the appearance of their books. In fact, they seldom even had any input when details such as cover illustrations were in the planning stages. Publishing houses employed graphic artists, designers, and layout experts to create an appropriate cover, pick the size of the finished book, choose the fonts, and handle the final typesetting and layout issues. Authors waited breathlessly to open that first box of books and discover the appearance of their creation. I remember that feeling well. Sometimes it resulted in a loud, wailing, "GAH!"

Every author over the age of forty probably has at least one sad story of a book gone astray at the hands of the publisher. Serious historical novels showed up with buxom women in low-cut ball gowns and bare-chested men flexing their muscles on the cover. I had one academic publication in which whole paragraphs lacked spaces between the words. The final straw for me came when *A Scratch with the Rebels* arrived in a large, two-columned page format that resembled a junior high school textbook rather than the scholarly history it was meant to be.

But whether we are happy about it or not, those days are long over. Publishers trying to stay afloat in their shrinking businesses have cut their staffs and services. Many authors now get to help with design features only because they work cheap. And for independent publishers, the entire burden is one they must handle for themselves. The results are not always pleasing. As Anatole pointed out to his fellow mice, the reputation of all independent publishers depends on the quality of whatever self-published book a reader picks up. If that book turns out to be full of typos, or lacks sufficient margins, or in some other way fails to live up to what a reader expects to find in a book, we all suffer a diminishing of our efforts.

Printer-Speak

The printing company you choose will provide you with the rules and standards you need to follow in preparing your manuscript. Chances are, however, that the technical terms they use will leave you confused. Here are some of the more common ones that the company will expect you to understand.

- **Bleed**—An image bleeds when it runs off the edge of the printed page. The condition occurs most often on your cover, where you don't want a white line to surround the artwork. The colors must go all the way to the edge. Most printers will allow one-eighth inch beyond the trim line for bleed, although some digital printing companies may need more. **The safe area** is the area that is far enough away from the trim or gutter edges to be considered "safe" from being chopped off within the tolerances of the printer's manufacturing equipment. The final size of the book is called the **trim size**.
- **CMYK**—Printers blend cyan (half way between green and blue), magenta (half way between red and blue), yellow and black inks to create all other colors. The image on your computer screen uses **RBG**, a combination of red, green and blue pixels. If you want your printer to use color illustrations, the images will need to be in CMYK.
- **Crop marks**—Lines on artwork, either digital or mechanical, intended to show where the reproductions should be cut to achieve the final trim size.
- **DPI**—Printers express the amount of information contained within an image file as its resolution or *dots per inch*. Computer monitors usually display screen images at 72 DPI on monitors, but printers typically require image resolutions of 300 DPI to produce acceptable results. That's why you cannot simply cut and paste an illustration from your computer screen to your printed page. You must provide the original file.
- **Grayscale**—This term is used to describe black and white graphic images. For book interiors intended to be printed only in black, all graphics should be grayscale.

- **Gutter, margin**—Margins are the blank spaces around the typed area on a book page, but printers call the inside margin the gutter, and it is always the margin on the bound edge of the book page. When you're looking at a book page spread, you'll have two gutters together, doubling the space in the middle. Keep in mind, however, that much of the gutter margin will disappear into the binding. Visually a page should show a white space of a half-inch to three-quarters of an inch on all four sides.
- **Justification**—Describes how the typesetter arranges the left and right margins of a block of type. *Flush left* type is even on the left margin and ragged on the right edge. *Flush right* is the opposite. *Justified* typesetting varies the amount of space between words (and sometimes between letters) to create straight margins on both the left and right sides of a block of type.
- **Pagination**—Printers call all right-hand pages the "recto" side (meaning the *correct* side), while they use *"verso"* (the back side) to refer to all left-hand pages. Recto pages always have odd numbers; verso pages have even numbers. All sections of a book must start on a recto, or odd-numbered page. If your chapter ends on an odd-numbered page, you will have one blank page between the end of the chapter and the start of the next one. The page number of the first page of every section is left blank, but the page still counts. So, for example, the first page of Chapter 1 bears no number but counts as page 1.
- **Running Head**—A header shows readers where they are in the book. Running heads (at the top of the page) or running feet (at the bottom of the page) can include the book title, author name, part title, chapter

title or subject headings to provide navigational help to the reader.
- **Serif**—Typefaces that evolved from calligraphic originals still show the influence of scribes writing with square-nibbed pens because they have serifs, a little finishing stroke on each letter. (Times New Roman, Georgia, Garamond) Type designs without these flourishes are **sans serif.** (Arial, Helvetica)
- **Widow/orphan**—The first or last line of a paragraph left at the bottom or stranded at the top of a page, usually considered an aesthetic defect in better typography.

You Can't Judge a Book by Its Cover

Do you believe that old saying? Well, think again. Oh, it may work if you're talking about the old lady down the street who scared off a couple of burglars with a few well-aimed shots from her trusty revolver. It may apply to the tattooed teenager with a ring in his nose—the one who surprised you by shoveling all your sidewalks after the first deep snowfall of the year. But if you're an author, don't believe this particular bit of advice for a moment.

Spend a little time in a book store, and you'll see why I say that. Almost without fail, customers will head first to look at the books with the biggest displays—the ones on a central table with a big "Best Seller" sign—or the multiple copies of a single title at the end of an aisle. Bright covers will also catch a customer's eye. The last place a shopper will look is a bookshelf where all the books have only their spines and titles showing. Next, watch what they do when they pick up a book to examine it further. First, they'll look at the front cover illustrations. Then almost immediately, they'll turn the book over to see what's on the back cover. Only the most inveterate readers will go on from there to open the book and examine what's inside. Sales decisions happen that quickly. Most buyers choose or reject a book by the cover alone. That observation may break your heart when you think of how long you spent writing your book, but you must not ignore the fact.

Does that mean that nobody cares what's inside your book? No, not exactly. It just means that no one will see the inside of your book if the cover does not arouse their interest long enough to get them to open the book.

By all means, start to think about your cover early. Readers are confronted with millions of choices when they look for a book, and your cover needs to be able to catch their attention quickly.

Try walking into a bookstore with no real purpose in mind. Just stroll around and notice which books catch your eye. Which ones fairly jump off the display table to say, "Hey!" and which ones make you curious once you have taken a closer look? Many factors go into book cover design, and unless you already have artistic ability or design experience, you may not immediately understand why some covers are better than others. Look at how many different elements appear in your favorite covers. Is there just one image or many? Are the colors a hint about the content? Does the cover image wrap around the book from front to back? Do you like cutouts? Embossing? Glitter? (Oh, I hope not!)

When you've found a few designs you like, try walking away from them and looking back at a distance. While seeing your book prominently displayed on a bookstore table is the ideal, how will prospective readers encounter it? Will it stand out from others of the same type? Will nothing but the spine be visible on the bookshelf? Will buyers go online and see only a thumbnail version? And if so, are the elements on the cover big enough to be visible in a thumbnail? All of these are issues you should understand before the actual design process begins.

But design it at this stage? Not so fast! Are you experienced enough to do your design? I know I wasn't. I had an idea of what I wanted to show on the cover, but it took a professional to do the actual positioning, the trim sizing, and the font selection. Depending on what company you choose to handle the production of your books, you may need to pay for their design services or hire a designer to prepare the cover copy for you. Don't scrimp here. A poorly designed cover can lose a prospective sale in just a few seconds.

Finding the right designer can be a challenge, of course, but here are some tips to help you on your search.

- Ask your fellow writers at the next book conference you attend. They may even be able to point out a good one standing just feet away from you.
- Look at published books in your chosen genre and read the acknowledgments or metadata to find out who did the cover.
- Check the internet for book cover contests. There are several of these every year, and you can look at the samples from many designers in one spot.
- Contact any potential artist and ask to see some examples of her work.
- And then, before you hire a designer, get to know her. How long will it take? How much will she charge? And is she open to suggestions from you? After all, you know your book better than anyone.

Front Matter

Once readers open your book, the Front Matter is the first thing they see. The following items may appear before the first numbered page of any book. These sections have lower case Roman numerals.

- **Title Page** [required]—The first printed page

displays the title and author's name, centered on the page. The Title Page is page i.
- **Copyright Page** [required]—This page contains all available copyright information (title, subtitle, author, publisher, date of publication, subject headings, Library of Congress designation, ISBN, and Library of Congress Cataloging Information). The Copyright Page appears on the back of the Title page and is always page ii.

After those two pages, you may want to include one or more of the following features. But don't overdo it. Your reader wants to get on with the story.

- **Dedication Page**—A personal acknowledgment of private debt ("For my mother, who believed in me") by the author appears on a single page, centered.
- **Epigraph**—A quote or saying to suggest the theme of the book.
- **Foreword**—A short essay typically written by someone other than the author. An opening statement by a well-known author or expert lends credibility and a stamp of approval.
- **Preface**—An essay written by the author explains how or why the author wrote the book.
- **Author's Note or Introduction**—an overview of the contents of the book. It may involve an explanation of how the author attributed sources, took literary liberties, referenced materials, or organized the content.
- **Prologue**—establishes the setting and provides necessary background information.
- **Acknowledgments**—A listing of those who contributed to the writer's efforts with assistance and

support. This section may appear in the back matter instead of here.
- **Table of Contents**—The listing of chapters includes page numbers.

Back Matter

After the last page of the manuscript's text, pagination continues in numerical sequence into the Back Matter. The Front Matter is paginated using lower case Roman numerals, but the Back Matter is not. The specific elements included at the end of the book should appear in the Table of Contents in the Front Matter.

- **Epilogue**—A final section provides narrative closure and serves as a final chapter to reveal the fate of the characters. It can also hint at a sequel or wrap up any loose ends in the plots or subplots.
- **Endnotes**—Citations to specific quotations in the body of the work appear at the end of the manuscript in this section. Endnotes must be listed numerically and consecutively in your manuscript and your endnote citations. Most readers, writers, editors, and publishers prefer endnotes to footnotes. Footnotes appear at the bottom of the same page as the citation of the work, whereas endnotes appear at the end of the manuscript in the Back Matter.
- **Bibliography**—A comprehensive list of any references cited in work. It is not a reading list on the subject. It must follow a standard such as APA (American Psychological Association) style, MLA (Modern Language Association) style, or University of

Chicago style. The bibliography should follow the same style as the manuscript and endnotes.
- **Glossary**—An alphabetical list of specialized vocabulary or terms and concepts that are relevant to the subject. Commonly used in works of non-fiction, some novels may come with a glossary for unfamiliar terms in a created world.
- **Appendices**—Tables, diagrams, maps, charts, photographs, and illustrations do not usually appear in a work of fiction. An author may choose to group all non-textual materials into Appendices. In the Back Matter, a list of appendices or figures provides titles, captions, and sources in numerical and consecutive order of their appearance in the book.
- **Permissions for copyrighted material**—Did you include a song lyric? A piece of artwork? A poem or a long passage excerpted from another book? Trademarked or brand names? Photographs? Fair use under the US Copyright Law does not apply because book publishing has a commercial intent. A list of copyrighted materials with attribution and credit noted is required. The terms of copyright permission may specify the conditions under which their work appears and may require a fee. A list of the copyright permissions appears in the Back Matter.
- **Illustration/Image credits**—photographs and other pictures with attribution and copyright noted. Even if your manuscript is entirely text, you may need to credit the cover image.
- **For Further Reading**—Depending on the nature of the book, the author may include a reading list or references of interest to a reader who wants to pursue an action or additional investigation.
- **Index**—Fiction rarely needs an index, whereas

nonfiction usually does. Prepare a list of index terms. Creating an index—the process of identifying the page on which each name, subject, or location appears—is a professional service, for which a publishing contract may require you to pay. It is also one of the last steps in the pre-production process of manufacturing your book. It cannot be finished until the final type-setting is complete.

- **About the Author**—If there is no dust jacket for the print edition, on which the author's biography typically appears, it goes in the Back Matter. Some authors include a list of their previously published books.

All Those Elusive Book Numbers.

If you want to sell your book in any retail outlet, whether it be a book chain, an independent shop, or an online source such as Amazon, or if you want your book in any library, it must have an International Standard Book Number, known as an ISBN. Every country has a single agency responsible for issuing ISBNs. In the United States, the company is Bowker Identifier Services.

Every book format must have a unique number. A new edition or a different format will require a new number. Originally ISBNs had ten digits. In 1998, companies expanded the numbers to a thirteen-digit form, with the first three digits being 978. That will remain the case for the foreseeable future, but it provides for the possibility of change if all available numbers are exhausted. The numbers have five parts of a variable length, each one sometimes separated by a hyphen. For now, the first three are always 978. The second section represents the country; the third, the publisher; the fourth, the title; and the fifth, a code number to verify the other sections.

Most printing/publishing companies will offer to provide your book with its ISBN, but that means that the book will have the publisher listed as, for example, Smashwords, or CreateSpace, or Lightning Source. If you want your own publishing company listed, you must purchase the ISBN directly from Bowker.

I had already decided that I wanted to publish under my imprint, Katzenhaus Books, not the book production company. Bowker was selling one number for $125.00 or ten for $250.00. It's a bargain, right? But at the end of months of writing, I had reached the "never again stage" and wasn't at all sure I would ever need more than one number. After agonizing a bit, I opted to order ten, all the time feeling ridiculously extravagant. As an update, the price in 2017 for one number remains the same, but ordering ten will now cost you $295.00.

Then I started checking on other matters. While I love print books and want my book to be an object people can pick up and examine, I also love my Kindle. And I'm hopelessly infatuated with the new iPad. I wanted my book available in all formats. So what difference did that make? Well, you don't have to have an ISBN for the Kindle edition, but you can provide one, and it's useful if you plan to issue in several formats. Do you want to distribute an Apple version? You have to go through Smashwords, a company that formats your manuscript for all e-book platforms other than Kindle. Smashwords requires an ISBN that is different from both the print version and the Kindle version. So I already needed three ISBNs for my single book. I saved myself $125.00 by ordering the set of ten.

Publishers—including self-publishers—register their company and contact information with Bowker and order anywhere from one to one thousand ISBNs. Then when they assign a number to a particular book, the publisher just goes to the Bowker website and registers the format and title in the appropriate slot. That guarantees that purchasers will be able to find the book and that *Books In Print* lists the book. Don't skip this step. The lack of an ISBN marks the book and its author as rank amateurs. Many bookstores also require books to have a printed barcode—also issued by Bowker. The barcode is a graphical representation of the book's ISBN and its retail price. If you use a professional cover designer, the company may provide the barcode as part of the back cover, so be sure to check that before you pay Bowker for one.

Copyright Law

Now, a brief word on copyright. Authors never need to pay for (or even register) their copyrights. Your copyright comes as soon as you write anything. So don't let anyone charge you for that copyright. Just make sure your manuscript has the all-important symbol: Copyright ©Your Name and Year of Publication. It goes on the second page, the reverse of your title. That's it. That's all you have to do.

It is possible, however, to register your copyright, if you so desire. Having the copyright registered provides an additional degree of protection if your book should ever end up in a court of law. For example, if someone plagiarizes your work and passes it off as his own, it may help to be able to point to the date on which you registered the copyright. You'll have to decide for yourself if the registration fees are worth it.

I didn't think so until my second book started to gain national attention and a screenwriter came sniffing around my copyright setup. Then I learned that $35.00 was a safeguard, particularly when I compared it to what a successful screen version of the book might earn. It is now possible to file your registration online and then mail in a copy of the book to complete the process. I recommend doing it.

You will also want to obtain a Library of Congress cataloging number, which guarantees that your book appears in the Library of Congress catalog for all time. Librarians want to see an LCCN so they know how to enter the book into their cataloging system. The publisher must send the first copy of the completed book to the Library of Congress, where a clerk will record all the necessary data describing the book and create an original catalog entry. Your production company may take care of that for you, although they will undoubtedly charge you a fee for doing so. CreateSpace will handle the process for $75.00.

As I recently discovered, it's quick and easy to do it yourself, although the explanations make it seem difficult. A two-step process asks you to prove to the licensing office at the Library of Congress that you are a real publisher. A one-page online application form takes just minutes if you have named your company and purchased ISBN numbers from Bowker. You will provide company name, your name and address, an email address, a website URL for the company website, and your ISBN identifier, which is the long six-digit number in the middle of your ISBNs. Although the instructions said an answer would arrive within a week, it took only an hour. By return email, they informed me that I was eligible and assigned me an account number and password. A link then took me to the next one-page application form, where I filled out the book information—title, author, and approximate length. And again, within an hour, I received my LOCC number. The final step will be to send them a copy of the book when it comes out. Easy, and so not worth paying someone like CreateSpace $75.00 to do it for you.

The Challenge of Book Layouts

Sometimes I suspect that today's great strides in technology have given us too much confidence in our ability to "do everything." My case in point? The current tendency for authors to assume they can produce a great-looking book by using nothing more than Microsoft Word, followed by saving it in PDF format. You've seen the results, I'm sure. The book fairly shouts "Amateur printer!" at you as you pick it up. Here are some of the things that can go wrong when a new author tries to do page layouts.

The text is difficult to read. Even if you avoid those cutesy fonts that are designed to look like a third-grader wrote them in chalk, it is all too easy to choose the wrong font for the right purpose. Fonts like Garamond or Baskerville use serifs—those little feet or flourishes at the ends of the letters. They are not there for decoration. They are designed to carry the eye from one letter to the next. When you're dealing with large blocks of text, they make reading much easier. Sans serif fonts, such as Ariel or Helvetica, are better suited to headings and chapter titles, where you want the individual word to stand out.

Pages look too crowded or show too much white space. Every font has slightly different spacing. For example, Garamond will require thirty percent more pages than Times New Roman to display the same document. Decisions about which to use depend on many factors, such as your intended audience, the number of internal breaks in the pages, the lengths of paragraphs, or predetermined page limitations.

Typesetting is flawed. The errors that can happen are almost too many to name. Margins change in width from page to page. Paragraph breaks have both a blank line and an indentation. (It is correct to do either one, but never both.) Underlining is wrong in any usage. Underlining is a printer's cue to set the type in italics. Underlining should never appear in the finished text. Straight quotes, like those from an old-fashioned typewriter, enclose spoken remarks. All publications now use curly ones instead. Right-hand margin is jagged rather than justified. Some lines are short because someone has tried to avoid hyphenation. Worse, the right-hand margins are justified, but some words have huge gaps between letters to stretch them to fit. W o r d s l o o k s t r e t c h e d.

Page numbering is off. Books follow many conventions that you may ignore at your peril. For example, the right-hand pages have odd numbers, and left-hand pages have even numbers. Cross them up, and you will confuse even readers who do not notice the actual numbering. Also, new chapters always start on a right-hand page. That means that if one episode ends on a right-hand page, the next page is left blank so that the new chapter starts correctly. If you have headers on each page, they should not appear on a blank page or the starting page of a new chapter.

If you learn those rules, will you be able to produce your book layout? That's still doubtful. My suggestions here will work for someone who only wants to turn out a few books, with limited distribution. I tried this myself, with a cookbook I put together for the Lions Clubs of Western Tennessee. Originally, I printed only 100 copies, sold them all to fellow Lions (mostly people who had a recipe in the book!), and raised $1000.00 for one of our local charities. Later I revised the text a bit and sold another 150 or so copies to Lions from out of state who were attending a conference in Memphis.

When I look at the book now, I am fairly pleased with its typography, although the font is childish. Page numbering is correct with justified margins, paragraph spacing is correct, and I managed to fill any white spaces with lots of cute little clip art (which now makes me shudder.) The book served its purpose, but no one looking at it would mistake it for a professionally-designed or published book.

I might recommend the Microsoft Word or Apple Pages book layout programs if you plan to produce a book of anecdotes for your class reunion, if you're helping your ten-year-old niece to "publish" her first short story, or if you want to preserve some family stories for future generations. If, however, you have written a beautiful story whose content can compete with professionally-produced books in its genre, don't spoil its first impression with an amateurish layout.

You have only two options, even today with all our recent improvements. If you plan to write several books—and if you are willing to invest a fair amount of money and the time needed to learn the newest software—Vellum (see Chapter 4) will do a credible job of typesetting your book and giving it that necessary professional finish. (Note: I formatted both the Kindle and print versions of this book with Vellum, so you can judge its quality for yourself.) If you do not wish to spend that kind of time or money, then hire a professional layout designer.

Getting Ready to Create Your Kindle Edition

I don't think it is possible to say this too often: Electronic books are not print books. They need a whole different approach to editing. Once you have finished editing your paper version and arranging the copy to appear attractively on the page, you can step back and admire it. Both edges are justified, and the lines are well spaced. No noticeable gaps appear in your words. If you've had a specialist do your layout, you can feel confident that no rivers of white space distract the reader. And best of all, that page layout will never change into a form you do not like.

None of that applies to an electronic book, simply because the nature of an e-text is to be fluid. One reason a lot of people like their Kindles lies with their ability to increase or decrease the font size to suit their own visual needs. I've touted that myself. But you understand what that means, right? Increase the font by two points and lines are no longer the same length. A hyphenated word may look fine in print, but come off very badly in an e-book, because the hyphen may now appear in the middle of a line. One early reviewer of *Beyond All Price* censured the book because she thought I had been trying to make fun of a speech defect by putting in random hyphens. The attack was so wrong-headed that Amazon pulled the review, but the experience warned me of the problems that can result from failing to examine an electronic version carefully enough.

Another source of trouble lies with hidden codes, such as spacing between words. Even if you turn on a program that lets you see the coding, the tiny dot that indicates a single space can be almost invisible. I strongly recommend that before you convert your text to any electronic format—and before you let someone else do the coding for you—you use the search and replace feature of your word processor to comb your document over and over again. You need to check these minor errors that can cause major problems.

- First, remove all automatic hyphenation. Only the person doing the final layout can determine when and if a word needs to be hyphenated. Leave the right justification to an expert.
- Next, look for hyphens used in place of a dash. We all use hyphens this way, I suspect. There's no em-dash key except in symbols charts, so we substitute a double hyphen. Sometimes, the newer word processors will automatically change a double hyphen to an em dash. But if yours doesn't, you will have to search for two hyphens and then do an automatic insert of the correct mark. You'll also need to note that when two hyphens separate numbers, an en-dash, which is slightly shorter, should replace them. But you're still not done. You also need to search for dashes with spaces on either side and remove those spaces. I know. I know! I like the appearance of the look, too, but it will not translate correctly to an electronic version. Trust me on this.
- Remove all tab stops, even those that you've been trained to use to indent the first word of a new paragraph. Indenting the first word of a paragraph with a tab stroke can cause horrible alignment problems on a Kindle. And don't substitute five spaces for a tab stop. That will only make the situation worse. The only safe way to handle indenting the first line of a paragraph is to designate it in the formatting feature of your word processor.

- While we're talking about spaces, do a search and replace for two spaces in a row, and automatically replace them with one space. My old typing teacher insisted on two spaces at the end of a sentence, but that is no longer the rule. You may know that, but your right thumb, which adds the spaces, will betray you if you are a good touch typist.
- Search for abbreviations and put them in small caps: 6 AM not 6 A. M. or 6 a.m. You'll find the small cap function under format and then font.
- Forget what your English teacher told you and put all punctuation marks inside quotation marks: ?" not "?
- And speaking of quotation marks, change all straight quotes to curly quotes. Then be prepared for more trouble. If you have had to use a single mark to create an apostrophe at the beginning of a word to indicate pronunciation, it will probably be curved the wrong way. You need to remember that the tail of an apostrophe always points to the left. Consider this sentence: *Y'all don't come from 'round here, do ya'?* Look at *y'all* and *don't* and then compare it with *'round*. To turn that curly mark around, you will have to type it like this: *a'round*. Then remove the a, and you get *'round*. For your sake, I hope you never even have the problem, but for me, it's a constant annoyance if I try to duplicate slave speech.
- Check your numbers to make sure you've used the numerals 1 and 0, not the letters l and o.
- Finally, check your hard returns (paragraph markers) to make sure you have not used more than one to create vertical spacing.

The process of cleaning up these tiny errors can be tedious and time-consuming, but it is a detail that marks the difference between an amateur and a professional. If you want your book to translate to an electronic version and still look good, take all the time this process requires.

Above all, remember that as an author, you have a responsibility to the entire writing community to produce the very best book you can possibly create.

CHOOSING THE RIGHT PRODUCTION COMPANIES

Silly old fox, doesn't he know? There's no such thing as a Gruffalo!

In Julia Donaldson's book *The Gruffalo*, quick-thinking Mouse takes a stroll through a scary woods. Along the way, he meets three animals who think of him as lunch. Each one invites Mouse to his house for a meal, but in each case, Mouse makes an excuse. He is going to meet his good friend Gruffalo, who is one-half grizzly bear and one-half buffalo, and they are going to dine on Gruffalo's favorite dish—Roasted Fox, Owl Ice Cream, or Scrambled Snake. The fox, the owl, and the snake all change their minds about having Mouse for lunch. As they run, fly, or slither off, Mouse makes fun of them for not realizing that the monster is not real.

Then comes a shock. The Gruffalo turns out to be real after all. The smart Mouse, however, convinces the Gruffalo that all the creatures of the woods believe that Mouse is the most terrifying animal of them all. The Gruffalo and Mouse walk back through the woods so that Mouse can prove his claim. When the fox, the owl, and the snake see them coming, they all run away. Then Mouse claims that his favorite dish is Gruffalo Crumble, and the monster flees.

What does this have to do with producing a book? Well, Mouse escaped danger by understanding what made each animal strongest and weakest. When you start to consider how to get your story out of your word processor and onto a bookshelf, you'll have several choices. Some companies will show you a package deal, offering to do all the production work for you for a one-time payment. Then there are print-on-demand companies, internet sites for electronic editions, and sound studios suggesting audio books. You can't make the right choice until you understand the pros and cons of each offer.

What Happens Now?

Let's assume you've finished writing your book and correcting all the mistakes. (Pretty big assumption there, but, hey, it has to happen eventually.) And I also assume you want to see it move from your computer screen to a real book that other people can read. That's why you wrote it, right? Now you're faced with more decisions, and making your way through the various options awaiting you will not be easy. Let's try to make it easier.

Your manuscript could take many shapes—a hard-bound book, a trade paper edition, a digital file for e-readers, an audio book, a large-print version, or maybe even a slide-driven lecture series. Start by eliminating the options on both ends of that list. If you are not a big-name author with a major publishing house funding your efforts, you can forget the first choice. Case-bound books cost too much to produce and carry too hefty a price tag for most readers. And if you're not that same well-known author, you'll have trouble convincing anyone to purchase an unfamiliar format such as the lecture series. That leaves three choices—trade paper, digital, and audio.

No matter what your final choices are, however, I can guarantee you that there are companies out there ready to pounce on your inexperience to offer you a deal you cannot refuse. Just mention on the internet that you have a book you'd like to publish, and they'll find you. Package deals that take all the work out of publishing and blue-sky promises of instant best-seller status will follow you everywhere. How to choose?

Who Believes This Stuff?

For one week recently, I kept track of unbelievable offers arriving in my mailbox. They're not rated as spam (YET!) by my reputable mail server, although it manages to find fifty to sixty other types of spam that it automatically removes for me. No, these appear to be genuine offers from talented and wise sources—until you read the small print.

In that one week, I received ten offers from promotion companies, all of whom seem to think I need business cards, brochures, posters, billboards, newsletters, and postcards to advertise my latest book. OK, I've used some of those products in the past, but when a company insists you buy at least five thousand business cards at a time, how many contacts do they expect you to have?

I also received three offers to let me access new collections of genealogical records at no charge all during the current holiday weekend. Apparently, they think their target audience includes lots of people with no place to go and nothing to do while others are partying. Still, the offer sounds generous, doesn't it? I checked out one of these. It promised to provide wills from millions of people in all fifty states. Did it fulfill that pledge? Well, I found a couple of listings from my family tree, but that's all there was—just a listing. A will exists for John Smith of Anytown, the site reported. Can I see it? Well, here's a picture of the listing. Now I'll have to travel to Anytown and have the County Clerk try to find the file for #584938720-138.

Another offers to help writers de-clutter and organize their publishing lives by keeping detailed records. They'll even send you the first seventeen worksheets for free. The forms arrive, fresh and colorful, as downloads you can print off as needed. For the most part, these worksheets have an interesting title at the top— "Things To Do," "Local Contacts," "Publishers," and "Agents"—followed by a page of blank lines. If you want additional information on how to fill the sheets, you'll have to pay to take the whole course.

Others are so-called *free* video courses. Turn up your sound and watch while we tell you how to:

- Market Your Book for Free
- Create Content Everyone Needs
- Create A Webinar
- Write a Blog by Filling in the Blanks
- Automate Your Book to Audio

Every one of them spends over an hour talking about other people's success stories. And at the end, you're told to accomplish your goal by ordering an expensive book, a course, or a private coaching session.

Here's the worst one I found. The seller was a college dropout who claimed to have written several best-selling books before he was old enough to drink. And for several thousand dollars, he offered to teach me:

- How to develop an idea for a book in thirty minutes.
- How to write that book in two hours.
- How to write, publish, and market any book in three easy steps.
- How to go from "no idea" to published author in ninety days.
- How to write a best-seller, even if you are bad at writing and can't type.
- How to earn a six-figure income instantly.

Uh-huh! Don't think I'll buy the Brooklyn Bridge, either.

Audiobooks: The Next Big Thing

A book you can listen to sounds like an excellent idea. It's the perfect solution for the blind or vision-impaired. Anyone planning to drive cross-country alone will welcome a way to break up the monotony of the open road. Truck drivers love audio books. Amazon, naturally, was quick to jump on the trend by providing a publishing channel for audio versions of books they already publish. ACX (Audiobook Creation) is an elegant, inexpensive, and easy way to turn your book into a listening experience. Or so it would seem.

Here's how it works. You must first confirm that you hold the audio rights. If you are not under contract to a publisher, you automatically are the rights holder. If the book has a publisher, you must check the contract to make sure you know what you have granted to that publisher. But as an independent author, we'll assume you hold the audio rights

You then go to the ACX website and create a profile for the title—including a description of the book and the kind of narrator you are hoping to find. You also provide a short excerpt from the book, which potential narrators will read and record as an audition. Choose this passage carefully, making sure that it includes any particular difficulties that exist, such as rapid-fire dialog among several characters or conversation in a dialect. Then post the book so that potential narrators can audition for you. You can also solicit suitable narrators for yourself by searching the ACX database by age, gender, accent, or reading style. And then you wait.

ACX will notify you when one of its thousands of narrators submits an audition tape. Listen to it carefully to decide if this is the right voice to read your entire book. You may also look up the candidate's profile and listen to other narrations by the same person. If you decide you are happy with the audition, you click on "Make an Offer" and tell the candidate whether you wish to hire him on a royalty-share agreement or whether you are offering payment at a finished hourly rate. You will set a deadline by which time the potential narrator must send you the first fifteen minutes of your book for a final review. You will also set a deadline for the finished product. If the narrator accepts your offer, you will send him the full manuscript immediately. You and your narrator will work out the exact terms of the final contract online, following the ACX guidelines. The contract does not become binding until you have received and approved that first fifteen-minute sample.

When the narrator finishes recording your audiobook, you must listen to the whole recording, following your manuscript and marking any needed corrections. You can ask for two rounds of corrections in all. When complete, you pay any agreed-upon fixed rate to your narrator directly. If you have chosen a royalty share, those payments will go to the narrator as they develop.

ACX handles all formatting and distribution through Audible, iTunes, and your Amazon pages. It will then be up to you to market the audiobook to your fans. You will receive monthly royalty payments via direct deposit as you specify.

Does It Work That Easily?

I chose to try out this format on my best-selling book, *Beyond All Price*. My choice of a production company was ACX, the Amazon affiliate, because they handle the contracts between author and narrator and do all the final formatting. I received auditions from several possible readers and selected a talented and experienced woman who seemed to be a perfect fit.

She agreed to do the job as a 50/50 royalty split. If I had offered to pay her on an hourly basis, the cost would have run into several thousand dollars. The going rate is around $300.00 per finished hour, and my book turned out to be fourteen hours long. It may also be helpful to know that a narrator usually takes five or six hours of effort to produce a single finished hour. In this case, the project stretched out for over nine months because the narrator had other paying gigs and concerts (she was also a professional singer) that took up her time.

When the audio files arrived for our audiobook edition of *Beyond All Price*, it was my turn to listen to it carefully—word for word—and look for any errors, omissions, or extraneous sounds. What a different experience it turned out to be! I've never used audio books—my eyesight is better than my hearing—so it had never occurred to me to do so. But I was impressed. The narrator is an accomplished voice-over actress, and she managed to make each of the characters come alive. She even managed a very believable cat.

When she meowed in one scene, my office cat raised his head and started looking around for an interloper.

The whole process was easy for me. All I had to do was listen to the tapes at the end to make sure there were no glaring errors, and I think we ended up with a great product. However, it has not sold. Maybe my readers are not the kind of folks who prefer audio books. They may not drive cross-country, or go to the gym, or do other mindless things that would give them the time to listen. If they travel by car, they may also have a spouse and children who aren't interested in historical biographies.

ACX sent the narrator and me seventy-five code numbers apiece, each of which would pay for a free audio copy. The idea was to distribute the codes to our friends who would then write reviews for the website. I soon learned that I couldn't give the audio versions away, even by running contests. I still have over fifty left. My narrator had the same problem. And then we realized that we would receive no royalties on those free copies. So we were exhausting our small readership by giving the product away. The result after six months of publication? There were exactly sixteen paid copies in circulation, and the narrator and I had each received payments of approximately $50.00 total. As I write this, the sales total has only risen to twenty-eight copies. I feel sorry for the narrator because she did all that work essentially for free. At least I only spent a few hours on the project.

One recent study has shown that people who buy audio books are looking for young adult novels, romance, mystery/thrillers, fantasy, or science fiction. My Civil War biography was none of those. Maybe audio books are a great innovation, and I just did a lousy job of marketing. Maybe I don't believe in audio books (I've never purchased or listened to one), and if you don't believe in something, you can't sell it. Maybe I'm just an old fuddy-duddy who's stuck in a rut, but I've gone back to writing the next book in a format where I know what I'm doing. I don't think I'll ever do another audiobook.

Choosing Your Printing Company

For every aspiring author, a shady book publisher waits to take those dreams and turn them into cash for their own pockets. You need to understand how book publishers can fleece you and how different types of presses work.

Vanity Presses have been around a long time. They will publish almost anything short of pure snuff-it pornography, so long as the author agrees to pay all expenses. The author keeps all rights to the book and retains all profits, but these deals come with the requirement that the author must purchase a large number of books up front. Unless you have an empty room that you can fill with unwanted books, steer clear of any deal that says, "We'll publish your book if you buy 3,000 copies or 30,000 copies at whatever price we want to charge you." The press gets the money for the books from the start. You must recoup all the expenses by selling the books yourself. How many friends do you have?

Subsidy Presses may sound like a better deal. They also charge the author for most expenses, although they may offer a few limited services such as marketing or editing. They retain all the rights to the books, and you get to sell them by sending people to the company to make their purchase. The company makes a huge profit, and the author gets a small royalty, sometimes as little as five to ten percent of the proceeds. On average, these companies only sell about forty copies per title, so don't expect to recoup your outlay.

Print-On-Demand sounds even better. Thanks to the miracles of digital printing, they create the books at the time of sale, so no one gets stuck with an unmovable inventory. However, many of these companies still collect high fees by offering package deals for their services. They may require you to pay them to do your cover, your layout, your editing, your press releases, and your marketing, and you get only a part of the proceeds of the sales. Most also insist on providing the book's ISBN, which gives them the rights to your book. Care to sell your soul while you're at it?

Picking a company to produce your self-published print books, however, turns out to be easy because there are only two consistently reliable choices. After I considered all the deals and one-time great offers, I could recommend only two print-on-demand companies—CreateSpace, which is the POD arm of Amazon, and Lightning Source, which is a branch of Ingram, the retail book distribution giant. Here's a breakdown of what they offer.

Because CreateSpace is a subsidiary of Amazon, you should expect its approach to resemble the overall Amazon business plan: find out what the customer wants and then provide it more cheaply than anyone else. Authors who turn to CreateSpace are looking for the easiest—and cheapest—way to take their book from a computer file to a finished book that looks and feels like the other volumes in a bookstore. These authors want to provide the company with the original manuscript, probably in .doc or .docx format. They are hoping someone else with better skills can turn that document into "a real book." That means that it will have an eye-catching cover, a page of copyright information, maybe a table of contents, attractive chapter titles, orderly page numbers, and adequate margins. It should be free from obvious spelling errors and grammatical goofs, and its pages should be pleasing to the eye, free from unexpected holes in the middle of the text or illustrations that are blurred.

CreateSpace usually meets those criteria. You can purchase services that you need, but you are not required to pay for anything you prefer to do for yourself. With CreateSpace, it is theoretically possible to have your books printed and distributed on Amazon.com at no charge. If you can provide them with a polished and formatted .pdf file, they will make the books available to you on a copy-by-copy basis for a small fee to cover the printing cost, and you can sell them for whatever the traffic will bear. You retain all rights. The GIGO principle (garbage in; garbage out) applies here. If you send them a flawless manuscript, they will produce a flawless book. If your submission is riddled with errors, you can expect the mistakes to be obvious in the book.

Now in the real world, you are going to need some services. For my first book, I chose to have CreateSpace do my layout and my cover, based on my rough design. I did the editing because I had extensive editing experience. Their charges were reasonable and below the costs I found when I checked for free-lance cover artists and layout designers.

I made one additional purchase, which I came to regret. I paid CreateSpace to do my press releases. The releases were sloppily done and showed little understanding of the book. I had to demand that they rewrite them several times before I was satisfied. The company then sent those releases out to a list of some 10,000 outlets—television stations, radio programs, newspapers, magazines, talk shows, and libraries. But out of the entire list of recipients, I received exactly one inquiry for further information. And it came from my local newspaper! That was a lesson learned the hard way.

Except for their press releases, however, CreateSpace was satisfactory. They were responsive when I had questions. I could reach a live person within a minute or two and receive expert advice from a member of the team working on my book. They sent two rounds of free proof copies and immediately responded when I requested last-minute changes. The books they turned out were completely acceptable. Once I made my corrections and approved the proof copy, I uploaded their simple PDF file. *Voila!* I had my books in six days! I've never felt a need to go elsewhere for my print copies.

Customers who use Lightning Source are also pleased, although this Ingram subsidiary offers fewer services than CreateSpace and expects its authors to do more of the preparatory work. They will only accept a manuscript in .pdf/X-3 format, which you have probably never seen because it is a sophisticated interface that the Big Five traditional publishers use. To produce the required file, the author must either hire free-lance designers or invest large sums and much time toward mastering Adobe Acrobat Professional, which will run close to $500 for the software alone.

The books that come from Lightning Source are virtually indistinguishable from those of traditional publishers. However, their high-quality standards come at considerable cost. Customers who have used Lightning Source without hiring outside help sometimes voice angry complaints. Instructions use technical language that is unclear and hard to follow. Advice or clarification is only available via email and requires two or three days for turnaround. Changes also carry a service charge. Quality, it would seem, comes only at a price.

New Kids on the Block: Ingram Spark and KDP Print

Two additional printing options have become available in the past year, and they may be viable alternatives. Both strike me as being hybrids—a crossover of the vast divide between print and electronic books. The new plans may indeed set the next standard for independent publications. They certainly fit into the pattern of consolidation that is happening in other industries. I can't say a whole lot about these options because I've not tried either one, but I can tell you what the pundits are reporting and what the new companies say they offer.

The first to break into the market was Ingram Spark. In case you've forgotten, Ingram is the largest book distributor in the country and the parent company of Lightning Source. Ingram Spark is the company's solution to complaints that Lightning Source is too expensive and too complicated. It promises a cleaner, simpler interface, allowing authors to submit files similar to those Lightning Source accepts for digital editions. Since I've not tried this program, I can't evaluate that promise.

They do, however, offer certain advantages. The Spark plan will produce either paperback or hardbound copies, and there's little difference in the costs between binding styles. That will be important to any author who hopes to place books in schools and libraries, which will usually purchase only hardbound books. Spark's shipping charges for international sales are also considerably cheaper than those of Amazon because they have several overseas production facilities. Disadvantages, customers tell me, include production delays of six to eight weeks and no Canadian facilities. There is also a restriction on crossover publication between Kindle and Ingram Spark. Authors who have offered a book on Amazon's Kindle Direct Publishing platform within the past twelve months cannot publish a hardback version of that book with Ingram Spark.

Now KDP Print is offering a new way to publish a print version of your Kindle Select book. This idea bothers me a bit because it seems to be undercutting CreateSpace, which is also a part of the Amazon family. KDP Print takes your Kindle publication and turns it into a printed paperback. From what I can tell, the author has few options about the appearance of that book. It uses the same files, the same cover, and the same descriptions and categories. It is, on the other hand, much quicker than Ingram Spark, and cheaper for American shipments. It is also available in Canada.

Both programs are changing rapidly, and they seem to be spurring one another on to greater and greater improvements. I cannot recommend one over the other. I would not use either one until they have had time to demonstrate their particular merits. I would remind authors, however, that the final decision on publishing must not rely solely on quick and inexpensive options. If self-publishing is ever to compete with traditional publishers, or if you hope for best-seller lists and big-name reviews, your printed books must meet the same high standards as the rest of the industry.

Digital Editions

Picking an electronic edition is more problematic because there are several variations in formatting and more rivalry as those formats struggle for dominance. Do you need to publish your book as an e-book? Won't that hurt your "real" book sales? Isn't there something perverse about writing a book and then selling it as something that is not a book? On one of the discussion lists I follow, the participants are discussing the dangers of publishing both hardback and paperback editions at the same time. That's dangerous enough, some say. Why complicate matters by putting your hard work out there in some electronic form that people can't even pick up? I've heard all these questions, and I understand the unwillingness to jump into a new-fangled technology. But please pay attention. You need to do this!

Why You Must Publish Electronically

I know how satisfying it is to pick up a beautiful book and be able to say, "Hey! I wrote this book." The thrill of finding your book in a bookstore—maybe on a table at the front of the store—is worth all the effort you put into it. But what is your goal? You write because you want others to read. If you want to keep your words secret, you need to get a diary and hide it under your mattress. If you want living, breathing readers who will engage with your ideas, you have to go out and find them where they are. And the truth is that more and more book lovers are turning to e-books as their reading choice.

I'm not going to go into all the reasons why people like e-books. Let's accept the fact that readers are turning more and more often to their electronic gadgets instead of carrying a book. And when they are looking for a good read, they have lots of choices. According to one calculation, there are more than 3.5 million books currently for sale in the Kindle Store with more joining the list at a rate of twenty thousand a day. With an e-reader, a customer can have access to an additional 1.8 million out-of-copyright books published before 1923. And they are free. With all those choices, who, except maybe your mother, would pay $25.00 for your real book?

The question is not whether to publish an e-book, but in what format. Should you go with Kindle, or Apple's iBook, or one of the other smaller readers? The answer is yes. Until the industry settles down and creates a single standard, you need to put your material out there in every available format. That sounds daunting. If you're a complete technological klutz, you can hire someone to do the formatting for you, but it's not all that tough.

Start with Kindle. Kindle editions appear as choices on Amazon.com, right along with your print edition, and many shoppers will find your e-book there. Kindle offers complete instructions on how to submit your manuscript in one of the approved formats. They accept Word files (.doc, or .pdf, or .rtf among others). Follow their instructions, and your book will appeal like magic.

Then turn to Smashwords. These folks take your .doc file and convert your work into all the different formats needed for second-tier readers, using something they call a meat grinder. They also handle the distribution of your files to the ordering websites of all of those different e-readers. There is no charge for that service, and they stand behind their work. Apple's iBook store recently tightened their standards for e-book coding and notified me that my version of *Beyond All Price* had coding errors. I forwarded the message to Smashwords, and they fixed the problem within hours.

The company makes their money by featuring your book on a separate page in their catalog. They take a small amount of the sales on their site as their profit. You get sixty to eighty-five percent of the sale, without doing anything except letting them put your work out there.

There it is. No difficult formatting. No inventory to clutter your dining room. No sales pitches to deliver. No advertising charges. No sales to handle. No shipping to arrange. Money comes in steadily and reliably every month.

Why wouldn't you do this?

What If e-Books Are Just a Fad?

The collapse of Barnes and Noble's Nook Books sent shock waves through the digital industry. Mainstream publishers worried that this was only the first in a series of disasters that would bring about the closure of the country's last large independent book store chain. Indie publishers, however, feared that the market for electronic editions was drying up. Could this mean that digital publishing was nothing more than a fad?

I was particularly concerned about the fate of my first book, *A Scratch with the Rebels*. I had received my semi-annual royalties from the publisher and was moderately pleased to see that the 2007 publication was still selling. I was less than pleased, however, with a note at the bottom of the account. "As of January 2, 2014," it said, "we are discontinuing all e-book projects." What!? I'm a staunch supporter of electronic books, and from what my royalty statement was showing me, the Kindle and Nook versions of this book were outselling the paperback version by several hundred percent. Just to be sure, I checked my Amazon listing, and found that it listed the Kindle version of *Scratch* as "currently unavailable."

I wondered if I could protest. I had used a traditional publisher, and their contracts are usually pretty airtight. This one posed severe penalties for anyone who tried to take back their publishing rights—a $500.00 penalty to start, followed by a bill for every expense the publisher had incurred while making the book available. Ah, but there was a slight loophole. If the publisher refused to publish, the rights would revert to the author.

Armed with that bit of encouragement, I sent an email to the publisher, asking if I could get the electronic rights back. The reply came within hours: "Certainly!" I had been expecting a long argument, but there was none. They had decided to get out of the e-book business. If I wanted to publish the electronic version, they would be happy to send me all their files. Wow! It was almost too easy.

Now I had to deal with Kindle. Amazon is super careful about rights violations, and this book was already listed in their files with the traditional publisher, even if it was "currently unavailable." My email to them explained the situation and asked what I would have to do to remove the old listing and replace it with a new version, bearing my publishing imprint. Once again I expected a hassle, and instead, I got a quick and easy answer. "We have removed all traces of the electronic version," it said. "Feel free to upload your new listing to KDP whenever you are ready."

The bottom line here? When in doubt, ask lots of questions. Turn to legitimate writers' websites and writers groups. Rely on the advice of experienced authors. Don't deal with any production company without a proven track record, and don't be fooled by pie-in-the-sky offers of instant success.

LEADING UP TO LAUNCH DAY

"If you give a mouse a cookie..."

What happens when you give a mouse a cookie? The next thing you know, he'll ask for a glass of milk. Then he'll need a mirror to make sure he doesn't have a milk mustache. When he looks in the mirror, he'll notice some straggly whiskers and ask for scissors and a comb to give himself a trim. After his whiskers and fur are in place, he'll need some new clothes to go with his improved appearance. He'll want to stroll around the block to show off his new appearance, but the exercise will make him hungry, and he'll ask for another cookie. And so we go full circle. Laura Numeroff has created a whole series of children's books around this idea. You can fill in the blanks and create your own.

The lesson to be learned from our cookie-loving mouse is this. If you give a reader a taste of your upcoming book, she'll come back for something more. You had better be prepared to follow through because readers are not easily put off. That's the principle that lies behind most book launch recommendations. You can start with an announcement of an upcoming book, but you can't stop there. Bringing out a book starts early and continues through a cover reveal, maybe a virtual blog tour to promote the book, early reviews, and a quick excerpt—all followed by the grand finale of the publication of the book itself. That may lead to book signings and talks to other writing groups. And then you have to be prepared for the inevitable reader's comment: "It was a great book. When's your next one coming out?"

I'll Never Be a Used-Car Salesman

I will be the first to admit that I am not an expert on promotions, nor do I want to be. I don't like selling anything, and I particularly hate a hard sell. I know I turn a deaf ear to anyone who tries too hard to promote a product, and I assume others do, too. But I also know that as an indie publisher, if I don't promote my book, no one else is going to step up and do it for me. So what I'm offering you here is my soft-sell approach—a plan that I can live with without feeling that I've sold my soul in the process.

An Early Start

Starting early means yesterday, and you're already late. But you can catch up with a little effort. If you followed the Second Mouse's advice in Chapter Three, you began to build an audience for your book before you wrote the first word. You have a small platform of social media contacts. You have a website, and you have your blog. All of those are channels through which you can get the word out about an upcoming book. This is no time to be shy or secretive. Let everyone know you are writing a book. Drop hints. Ask questions. Share discoveries. Admit problems. Invite input.

People who share your efforts through Facebook or Twitter or word of mouth will appreciate and own the results. Here's one small example. I have become close friends with a young couple who help me with the weekly chores (like litter-box cleaning) associated with having three or four cats in the house. One day, while they were here, I complained about a writing problem I was having. I make a habit of writing a dead mule into every book (but that's another story!). In my current work-in-progress, I had managed to include the usual animal but couldn't find a way to kill him off without being messy about it. "Push him off a gangplank or a dock," the young man suggested. Now he's eager to read the new book to find out how I used his idea.

Newsletters are a great way to stay in touch with your readers between books. If you send a fan an email, you'll make her feel valued and increase the chances that she'll come back to read another book. The free program at MailChimp offers a smooth and impressive way to create a newsletter, but it's up to you to gather a mailing list. That can be tricky because more and more internet users are reluctant to pass out their email addresses. However, you have some built-in ways to collect your mailing list if you have followed instructions and stayed active on the internet.

Your website provides a good way to stay in touch with potential readers. If you add an "Opt-In Box" to your landing page, you can collect email addresses and then use them to pass along insider information about upcoming publications. Be careful how you set up the box. Place it on the opening page of your website, and position it at the top of the page where everyone will see it. Don't ask for more information than necessary. You don't need to know your readers' names, and you certainly don't need their addresses. You may want to include a promise that you will not sell or distribute the email addresses. Promise not to overfill their mailboxes. Some marketers suggest you offer a short story or something else free in exchange for the email address, but I am reluctant to do that. It feels like a bribe. Instead, I offer periodic updates on my writing progress and insider tips on the publishing industry. That assures me that those who send me their email addresses want to read the newsletters I send them.

Blog posts offer another source of reader contacts, although I have had limited luck with the practice of allowing online comments. Helpful comments sometimes appear. But so do nasty attacks and long pitches by people who take advantage of a free posting avenue to advertise their services. After a long siege with scammers who tried to hijack my blog in that way, I added a delay that allowed me to read all comments before they appeared on the blog. That helped, but it took more time than I was willing to devote to the task. I have now blocked all comments on my blog while letting people know that if they have questions or suggestions they can email me privately. That has taken care of the worst of the internet trolls who were taking advantage of my site to lure customers to their own businesses.

Add Some Different Social Media Sites

As soon as you have a final version of your manuscript, it is time to explore some new ways of bringing it to the world's attention. To do that, you're going to need help from some clever folks whose business revolves around promoting other authors' works. Here are the book sites I've found most useful. Goodreads has close ties to Amazon and will share their reviews. BookBuzzr provides marketing help in the form of gadgets you can add to your social media pages to advertise your books. AskDavid collects reviews from other sites and provides buy links for every book registered on the site, but also lets you tap into its enormous Twitter database to promote the latest news about your book.

Goodreads may be the most important because it has the biggest audience. You can sign up as a reader or as an author, but actually, you need to do both. As a reader, you compile lists of your favorite books (and you can go back as far as you like into your reading past.) For each of those books, you have a choice of giving the book a star rating, indicating how much of it you have read, or writing a full review. You can create bookshelves to organize your lists—My Favorite Books, Books I Want to Read, Recommended Reading, Ones I Couldn't Finish, Childhood Favorites, Waiting on my Nightstand. I've seen a few reader pages that sport a "Stinkers" shelf, but it's best to avoid such labeling. The authors of those stinkers are likely to retaliate against your books, so beware. If you encounter a bad book, the best policy is to ignore it and leave it off your lists entirely. Many Goodreads users don't include any book to which they would give a one-star or two-star rating. You'll also have a chance to send recommendations to your friends, to read other members' book discussions, or to set a reading goal for the year and then track your progress.

On the right side of the Goodreads home screen, you can start finding friends. The app makes it easy to tap into your lists of friends on Facebook or Twitter to see who is already a member of Goodreads. With those folks as your starting point, you'll soon be drawing friendship invitations from friends of friends, as well as strangers who have seen your recommendations. They, in turn, may draw you into discussion groups where you'll meet more like-minded people. See how your platform can grow!

The real heart of Goodreads, however, lies in how writers use it to draw attention to their new publications. When you declare yourself as an author, you'll get a new page. There you can take and answer questions from other members, post all of your books with full information, collect reviews, link to your blog posts, see all the stats on your ratings, and offer giveaways to promote your new book—all surefire way to entice new readers. And the best part of the efforts you put into Goodreads is that you already have a built-in audience, for it is a ready-made community of book lovers.

Bookbuzzr is a different kind of author site. For a reasonable monthly fee, it provides a set of book marketing tools that work behind the scenes while you are busy with other matters. That's important! You can get a widget or a full-screen page flipper that plays on your Facebook page or elsewhere and lets visitors sample your book in a realistic, page-turning fashion. You can schedule tweets for your books that play automatically as often as you like at whatever times you choose. Another perk allows you to design a book signature that you can attach to all your emails. You'll also get a full author page with your profile and biography, plus a listing of all your books, including buy links of your choice. The program will notify you if your Amazon sales rank goes up. It's like having a personal assistant working for you full time.

AskDavid is a third type of book promotion site. You join for a six-month period at a time and can enter as many currently-published books as you happen to have. The site collects reviews from various sources on the internet and posts them on your book pages so that customers do not have to hunt around for recommendations. It also allows readers to post their reviews directly on the site and provides a buy link to whichever dealers you choose. The added benefit here is that Ask David has a large following, and the site will post promotional tweets for your free book offers. It also encourages members to retweet posts about each other's books by providing more free tweets to those who retweet. You can use these additional links to this account for almost any other book-related announcement you may choose.

These are all opportunities I have used successfully to get the word out about my books. You can start by joining all these sites as a reader, so do that now, long before your book comes out. Then, when the final version of your book is ready for public consumption, you can quickly assume your status as an author and take full advantage of what the programs have to offer.

The Importance of Author Pages and Categories

Sometimes it's easy to overlook the other little things Amazon offers to help their authors get more exposure for their books. Although it doesn't always feel as if Amazon cares about the writers of the books they sell, they fully realize that authors are the people who provide their bread and butter. Amazon offers everyone who sells a book with them an individually designed author's page. These pages are an invaluable resource, and you should take advantage of the opportunity as soon as you can.

As soon as you have listed your first Kindle edition, even as a pre-order, you qualify for an author page. The goal of any author's promotion is to draw attention to her books, and what better place to do that than on a website that sells some seventy to eighty percent of all books, whether you're looking for hardback, paperback, or e-book.

Qualifying for an Author Page is simple. Do you have a book for sale on Amazon? Then you qualify to build your page. Just go to https://authorcentral.amazon.com using your Amazon ID. Amazon will provide a detailed bibliography of all your books, complete with links to each one's sale page. You then can add everything you want a prospective reader to know about you and your work.

Start with an appealing biography, and then add pictures of yourself (particularly at book-signings or speaking engagements), a list of awards you've received, your book trailers, links to your blog posts, your Twitter feed, and your schedule of events and appearances. You'll be given a link to your page so that you can tell anyone interested. Mine, by the way, is amazon.com/author/carolyn-schriber. Amazon will help you post that address on other social media sites if you choose. Keep the information updated regularly, and your readers will follow you with ease. They'll even find a button that will allow Amazon to send them a notice whenever you publish something new.

But wait! There's more. Author Central also provides you, the author, with another private page, purely for your use. When you sign into Author Central with your Amazon ID and password, you will find a link to your author page, so that you can add information. Then you get a list of all your books so that you can check for completeness and accuracy. The Sales Info tab takes you to sales reports and book and author rankings. And the tab of Customer Reviews lists every review you receive on any book on Amazon (very useful when you're just curious to see if there has been a new review. You can have them shown by title or by date received.)

These two pages give you everything you need to sell your books on Amazon. It's a one-stop promotion headquarters. Yes, there are other places to list your book on the internet, but this is the most important one. It's accurate, it's kept up-to-date (every hour!), and it's free. Don't neglect it.

Another prime example of a hidden jewel is CreateSpace's Gallery of Previews—a marketing site that anyone who has a book listed on Amazon can use You don't even have to have used Create-Space as your source for print editions. Just go to createspace.com and log in with your Amazon ID and password.

- On the left, you'll see a listing for "Manage Previews." Click it, and you're on your way.
- Start by listing your title, your name, and a brief (300-character) blurb about the book.
- Identify the genre and pick an approximate date of publication. (If the book is already available, choose "today.")
- Next, choose a good, readable excerpt from the book—an interesting passage, a cliffhanger, a car chase if you have one—something to catch a reader's attention and make him want more. The selection can be a lengthy passage (around 25,000 characters if I remember correctly).
- Add an image. Ideally, this would be the cover of the book, but if you haven't decided on a cover yet, use a picture that illustrates the central theme of your story.
- And finally, add a few questions that a viewer might answer. For instance, "Did this chapter make you want to read more?" What you're looking for here is some feedback, as well as a blurb or two you can use later.

Long before your book comes out, you can prepare answers to some questions you will be asked about your book. Don't get caught off-guard when Amazon asks for a 4000-word description of your book the night before it goes live on their website. You must have the following information at your fingertips:

- Full Title
- Name of the Series, if this is one of a set.
- Author's Preferred Name and that of other contributors like the co-author, the illustrator, your editor, your photographer—any one to whom you have given credit for part of the book.
- Full Name and contact information for the publishing

company. If you are an indie writer, that's your small business, not the printing company.
- ISBN (both 10-digit and 13-digit) and any other numbers that identify the book, such as a Library of Congress Control number or other cataloging information.
- Description of Contents (The usual 4000 words is an upper limit, not a requirement).
- Brief Description (should be limited to 300-400 words to be used in catalogs).
- Keywords (Up to seven choices; these are words that readers might list in a search for a book like yours: Charleston, South Carolina, cotton, Civil War, women's rights, romance, family).
- Categories (Two choices. See discussion below).

You'll need to be particularly careful in choosing categories and keywords, for these largely determine your sales rankings on Amazon. If you select a broad category with thousands of books, it will be difficult to break into the top 100 best-selling books. If, however, you can find your niche in a small category, it will be relatively easy to achieve a high ranking. Also, note that Amazon is notorious for believing in its own propaganda. The sales rank tells you only how you rate in comparison to other books like yours. But once you achieve a high score, no matter how you come by it, Amazon will start promoting your book more vigorously, thus making the rank self-fulfilling.

Take my *Yankee Reconstructed* as an example. Obviously, it is Fiction, but if I choose Historical as the next level, I'm through. If I choose Afro-American, it then breaks down again, and I can pick Historical at the third level. What's the difference? In the first example, the algorithm on which Amazon works comes into play only when someone searches for the term Historical. In the second, the same algorithm will respond to either Historical or Afro-American. That could bring me twice as many hits.

Next, choose seven additional keywords. Amazon search engines will already be using any word that appears in your title and any of your categories, so you want to avoid repeating those. Again, you'll want the keywords to be relevant to your content and as descriptive as possible. Try to use single words rather than phrases. In the case of keywords, a phrase like Civil War will not trigger unless both words appear in the search criteria. Using War, however, would include the Civil War.

Pre-Orders

Several years ago, Amazon and other e-book retailers made it possible for independent publishers (like me) to take pre-orders for a new book, just as they do for traditional publishers. The hope is that there will be enough pre-orders to kick-start the book's climb through the rankings. How does that work? Retailers accept the orders but do not charge them or record them as purchases until they enter all those pre-orders in one batch on launch day.

I tried this for my first historical novel, *Damned Yankee*, which appeared on May 1, 2014. I was not impressed with the outcome. Yes, a few of my faithful readers dutifully pre-ordered their copies because I asked them to do so. I had the book on pre-order for a solid month, and there were only seven pre-orders on Kindle, and none on Apple or Nook as far as I could tell. Some of my readers didn't like doing pre-orders, and several said so. Readers did not gain a single advantage by making a purchase early. Unlike a product whose supply might disappear before you could get to the store, e-books never run out. So the book release did not cause any wild mob of lined-up buyers at the time. On the morning the book went live on Kindle, the seven pre-orders all came in at once, and they had no impact on the book's ranking. A couple of months later, the book took off well on its own and sold hundreds of copies a month for the rest of the year. The pre-order option turned out to be another waste of my time.

Would I bother doing it again? At the time, I thought not. However, I keep giving it a try. The next year I had a book coming out right after Christmas, and I was afraid the excitement of the holidays would make even my faithful readers forget about it. This time I tried to make sure the purchaser received something of value by placing a pre-order. I offered several incentives.

Why would readers want to order a book in October if they wouldn't get it until January? Well, first, there's the simple matter of forgetfulness (and that's something that happens to everybody, not just us seniors.) Between the first mention of an upcoming book and January came that whole holiday season, with all of its distractions. And when January arrived, potential readers were going to be exhausted, if not hung-over. Would they remember to order my book on January 3rd? Probably not. But if they had pre-ordered it, it would arrive just in time to fill that empty void that follows the holiday season.

Here were a few other advantages to pre-ordering. Most pre-orders carry a reduced price tag. My *Yankee Reconstructed* was available for pre-ordering at $3.99 on all the key e-book retailer sites: Apple iBooks, Barnes and Noble, Kobo, and Kindle. On January 3rd, the price would be $5.99, so readers could save $2.00 by ordering early. What was even better, they didn't have to pay a thing until the book shipped. So they could order it in October, and by the time the bill arrived in January, they wouldn't even notice that they were paying for it.

Next, I added another carrot. If customers sent me a copy of the confirmation email they received when they placed a pre-order (on any site), I entered their name into a "Happy New Year" drawing. One lucky winner would receive an autographed trade paper version of the novel, complete with matching bookmark.

Not enough of an incentive? Try this one, I begged the reader. Let's suppose you have a history-loving friend who enjoys historical novels, and you want to give her a book for Christmas. She might enjoy my novel set in the period of Reconstruction, but it won't be out in time for Christmas. With a pre-order, you can ask me to send her a Christmas card that will announce the "gift-to-come." It will have a picture of the book, the date of arrival, and include your name as the giver. Problem solved, and you don't even have to wrap the gift.

I also tried to be honest. I get more out of a pre-order than a reader does, at least in the short term. To understand why, you have to understand the methods by which companies compile "Best-Seller" lists. Every organization has its algorithms, but the idea is the same. The more copies a book sells, the more copies it will sell in the future. And since most of these lists appear every week, if not every day (or in the case of Amazon, every hour), the most recent sales take on an enormous importance.

Here's how the sellers count pre-orders. Sales don't get charged—or paid for—until the day of publication. So for several months, the pre-orders can pile up. And if a whole lot of people have pre-ordered the book, it will zoom to the top of its category ratings on the day that those sales all hit the cash register at the same time. Pre-orders have the ability to create instant best-sellers. So when you buy a book matters more than the mere act of buying it. That's why pre-orders are so important. They are some of the kindest gifts you can give your favorite author.

When I was ready to publish *Henrietta's Journal* recently, I did an intense campaign to get pre-orders during the last day or so before the launch. This time, when I stressed what a difference the pre-order number could make, readers responded. The number tripled in the last few hours, and, as predicted, it immediately pushed the book's sales ranking into the top one percent of all Kindle books on offer. Success, right? Well, not so fast. Most readers who had been waiting for the book pre-ordered it, and then there were no more sales on launch day. Those high ratings faded quickly. The overall effect was negligible.

So, does offering a new book as a pre-order work? I have to admit that I don't think it makes a whole lot of difference. I still do it, however, for a couple of reasons. I have a few faithful fans who love doing pre-orders. So for them, I keep the possibility open. I also find that the pressure of getting a pre-order ready is good for me. Amazon and Smashwords both want to see a finished manuscript of the product before they will announce it on their pages. That pressure makes sure that I finish the book in time to meet their deadlines.

I'll add one precaution, however. The last time I checked (and these rules do change), you could list a book on Amazon up to six months before its publication date. Smashwords will let you do it even earlier. But what's the point? Both digital platforms seem to be copying the practice of the Big Five hardback publishers, who have a different incentive for getting pre-orders. It tells them how big a print run they need to provide. Digital publishing does not need that kind of notice. Our books are ready in a day. I now open my pre-orders about a month in advance. If a reader is going to take advantage of a pre-order, that's plenty of time.

The Media Kit

Think you're ready to publish? Not so fast. One crucial step awaits your action. Just like the famous tree that falls in a forest without making a sound, so it may go with your book. If no one knows it's about to launch, no one will hear about it. You have to blow your own horn and make your presence known. Make no mistake here. I'm not talking about advertising. I'm describing publicity. You can pay to advertise your book. You have to earn your good publicity. Please keep that distinction in mind when you create a new press release.

A good press release has great potential for attracting readers to your book, but it requires several contributions from you. It must be newsworthy. You must include all details clearly and concisely. More important, the article must be formatted correctly so that the recipient sees it as a professional presentation. Here are some suggestions on how to do that formatting, so that everything fits on a single page.

- At the top of the page, put the words "FOR IMMEDIATE RELEASE" in all capital letters. That gives the columnist permission to use the information that follows. Skip a line and give the release date and the city of origin: "July 4, 1776, Philadelphia."
- Skip another line and write your headline. Keep it short and attention-grabbing. Type it on one line with the first letter of each word capitalized: "Patriots Declare Independence From England."
- Next, write a summary paragraph of about three to five lines, answering the standard questions: "Who, what, where, when, and why."
- Further information appears in the body of the press release. Include a plot summary, background information, and other relevant details. Keep this section to two or three paragraphs, each no longer than eight lines, and separate the paragraphs with a blank line to make them easier to read. Be sure to write this section in third-person point of view. Imagine that you are the columnist, and see the information through her eyes.
- End with contact details: the name of the publishing company, their media contact person (who is probably YOU!), a phone number, a mailing address, and an email address. A fax number or website may also be

useful. Make it as easy as possible for the reader to contact you and get more information.
- Close with one of the printing symbols that lets journalists know they have reached the end: —30— or ###

Once you have written your press release, the final task is to get it into as many hands as possible, but make sure that they are the hands of people who will have a legitimate reason to care about your announcement. You'll find many offers from public relations people to handle your press releases and send them out to their standard lists of thousands of publications. Such services are not cheap, but they are all too often worthless. Newspapers, libraries, radio and TV stations, alumni associations, and trade groups are all fair game for press releases, but only if you have some personal connection to them. If you live in Wyoming, a morning talk show on a Georgia TV station will probably not invite you as a guest. If you graduated from the University of Tennessee, the University of Florida does not want to hear of your accomplishments. On the other hand, your local high school or college newspaper may be looking for stories about alumni who have become famous. Your company headquarters may be proud to publicize an employee who has received an honor. Contact every news outlet within an hour or so's drive from your home, and make your availability clear. Use your writing talent to gain that all-important publicity. It lasts much longer than an ad.

But you are still not through. The press release is a great first step, but if it is to be useful, it must end up in a media kit with several other items. Remember those manila folders you used in school—the ones with pockets inside the folder? Here's the grown-up use for them. You ought to have at least six of these on hand for anyone who asks for one. And who will ask? Maybe that newspaper columnist, the local librarian who is thinking of inviting you to give a talk, or the book store manager who is considering letting you do a book-signing event. The goal of a media kit is to make the lives of these people as easy as possible so that they see you in a favorable and professional light.

The media kit starts with a copy of your press release, of course. Then add a full-page photo or two—your head shot, and the cover of your book are two necessities. A sell sheet is also necessary. It should include your name and the title of the book, a small picture of the cover, the metadata (publisher, date of release, ISBN), a short description of the book, and if possible, a blurb or two from a favorable review. It ends with full purchasing and ordering information.

Add Some Early Marketing Ideas.

I am not a fan of complicated or get-rich-quick advertising schemes, particularly when they come from promoters with big promises and big price tags but little to offer except a plan that once worked for someone somewhere. I've seen several of these that look like nothing more than a variation of the old pyramid scheme. Avoid them, no matter how often they invade your email. I am also wary of advertising offers from the major social media sites. They all seem to follow a pattern of charging you by the number of people who see your ad or how many clicks your ad generates. The problem with that approach is that you are forced to guess what those numbers will be without any knowledge or experience to guide your choices. It's all too easy to make mistakes and run up high charges without seeing any profits in return. My policy is to stick with simple promotional materials and postings.

You'll almost certainly need some inexpensive handouts. Start with a business card, and don't go anywhere without some cards in your pocket. A printing company like Vistaprint can do these quickly and professionally for you without breaking your budget. Watch their ads, and you can sometimes get as many as five hundred cards for under $10.00. Your card should contain just enough information to allow the recipient to contact you. Include your preferred name (probably not a nickname), your company name, an email address, and the URL of your website. Add your address and telephone number with caution to protect your safety and the security of your home. I use a post office box number rather than my street address and include only my cell phone, not my land line. Have a company logo? Make it part of the design. Keep the artwork simple so that it does not obscure the information on the card. One workable design plan is to have your contact information on one side of the card and your book cover on the other.

Another favorite idea is a bookmark that matches the cover of your book. Distribute the marker in every paper copy you sell, of course, and hand them out at talks or workshops, even if a reader only plans to purchase the electronic version. I usually try to pull some element of the cover picture to feature on the bookmark. For *The Second Mouse Gets the Cheese*, the first edition of this book, I used a chunk of Swiss cheese, with the cover mouse peeking over the top. The cover of *Yankee Reconstructed* showed the ruins of a South Carolina church that featured prominently in the book. The bookmark was a single column from that church. These should not have all your contact information on them. Limit yourself to book title, author, publisher, and date, along with the URL of the website. Vistaprint does not do bookmarks, but I have been quite satisfied with UPrint.

Your Elevator Speech

"Tell me about your book." You'll be flattered when someone expresses an interest in your writing, and you'll be tempted to launch into a full description. If the person is kind, he may hear a bit, but most people today—an agent, reader, publisher, bookseller or organization seeking a speaker—all want concise reasons why they would be interested in your book. They are thinking, "So what? Why would I want to buy it?" You don't want to bore your prospective readers or turn them off with too much detail. What they want is a quick summary of your book—your 30-second elevator speech.

Why is it called an "elevator speech?" Imagine that the encounter takes place in a moving elevator. You have only the time before the door opens again to make your sale. Without a 30-second description that states the book title, the intended audience, the main benefit to the reader, and what makes it unique, you lose the opportunity to give someone a reason to buy. You can also use this one as a two-sentence blurb at any business meeting or appointment where you only have a few seconds to impress.

What you include in your speech will depend on the book itself and the identity of the speaker. If the book is non-fiction, it will be easy to state the contents—"a history of . . ." or "how to . . ." If you're pitching the book to a publisher, you'll want to emphasize its audience. If you already know something about your listener, you can tailor the benefits to meet his needs At a convention of novelists, for example, you could quickly describe the conflict and crisis.

You'll end up creating several elevator speeches before you find one that works in most situations. When you're satisfied, practice it until it comes automatically. Here are some examples of where to start.

For a non-fiction title or a book like my own *Beyond All Price*, I usually concentrate on the subject.

- State the title. You want the listener to remember it once he steps off the elevator. Example: "*Beyond All Price* . . ."
- Describe the intended audience, making sure it will appeal to the listener. Example: "*Beyond All Price* gives people interested in the Civil War—whether professional historian or history buff—a clearer

understanding of what life was like for an army nurse during that tumultuous period."
- Add a few significant benefits if the elevator is still moving but be prepared to stop.
- Example: "*Beyond All Price* gives people interested in the Civil War—whether professional historian or history buff—a clearer understanding of what life was like for an army nurse during that tumultuous period. Nellie Chase's experiences expose her to the limitations of medical knowledge, the ongoing problem of what to do with former slaves, and the restraints placed on a woman by nineteenth-century social customs."

If your book is a novel, you may want to emphasize plot and character rather than benefits, So here's another outline:

- Describe the lead character. Example: "Nellie Chase is an abused wife . . ."
- Set the situation. Example: "Nellie Chase is an abused wife who signs on as a nurse with a Union Army regiment during the Civil War."
- Establish her goal. Example: "Nellie Chase is an abused wife who signs on as a nurse with a Union Army regiment during the Civil War. She is hoping for a new start, one that will allow her to atone for past mistakes and give her life a purpose."
- Who or what is the villain that stands in her way? Example: "Nellie Chase is an abused wife who signs on as a nurse with a Union Army regiment during the Civil War. She is hoping for a new start, one that will allow her to atone for past mistakes. A narrow-minded chaplain tries to drive her out of the regiment by

questioning her morality and forces her to find her life's purpose in an even more challenging role."

Whichever approach you decide to use, you will be ready for that quick moment when a sale or a contract depends on what you say in the next thirty seconds.

LAUNCHING AND MARKETING

"Who's the Leader of the Club That's Made for You and Me?"

Who better to lead us through the thickets of book marketing than Mickey Mouse, who transformed a small-time cartoonist into the titan of a worldwide empire? The nerdy-looking rodent in the short pants started out in black and white, but with the advent of colored film, he changed to bright red shorts and big floppy yellow shoes. He's closing in on being ninety years old now, but he's still going strong and changing as the world around him changes. One survey has found that ninety-eight percent of children ages three through eleven around the world recognize him. He has created movies, songs, fan clubs, a hit television program, merchandise, theme parks, and a global communications network. Scholars of popular culture have written dissertations about him.

So what can you learn from Mickey Mouse? Well, putting it in its simplest form, Mickey's creator, rather like Amazon's founder, found out what his audiences wanted from a cartoon character, and then he gave it to them. When vaudeville was all the rage, Mickey gave his audiences slapstick. When children began to idolize him, Mickey made sure that his behavior was always moral and respectable. And maybe most important, he let his followers escape from their daily lives into a fantasy world where everyone is happy and innocent.

And then—circle this in red—he sold that world to us. The Disney trademark reaps millions of dollars from Mickey Mouse's enterprises. Mickey doesn't shy away from putting a price tag on the enjoyment his fans derive from contact with him. He knows he has something of value, and he's willing to bet you'll pay to get it, too. If you're serious about becoming an author rather than a closet writer—if you're willing to put your words out there for the enjoyment of others—then you must also stand behind your books and claim their full value. Mickey Mouse would tell you that marketing your book is an essential part of the author's job.

Look How Far You've Come

Congratulations! If Mickey were here, he'd offer you a "high five." Just think of what all you've accomplished. You started your own publishing company and sharpened your business skills. You carved a niche for yourself in the massive world of social media and met people from all over the country. You tried new software and experimented with different writing styles. You created characters who came alive on your pages and gave them a story arc to travel. You discovered new ways to do your research and reviewed all those old lessons from your high school English teacher. (She's proud of you, by the way.) You evaluated offers from book production companies and learned some "printer-speak." You hired professional designers to give your manuscript a beauty treatment and reached the goal you set for yourself—a published book. Now it's time to step back and celebrate for a few moments.

Throw a Launch Party

The day your book goes live on Amazon or the day that the first carton of trade paper books arrives at your door is a day you will always remember. It's rather like a birthday, for this is the day you become a published author. It's time for a birth announcement, because creating a new book is rather like having a baby—months of discomfort, inconvenience, and agonizing pain, followed by the sudden appearance of a new creation that will change your life forever. It's time to throw a party.

You may want to make your celebration a real party to which you invite all your friends and family who have watched the months of labor you've put into your efforts. Choose a location that can be open to the public if you like. Sometimes your local bookstore or library will be willing to play host because you will be bringing in new customers. But don't limit your choices. Think about places that have a connection to your story. I've heard of launch parties at country clubs and retirement home event centers. Try the fire station, a beauty salon, a tea room, a gift shop, a bakery, a small local museum, a church basement.

If you are holding your party anywhere beyond your living room, you need to think about your host as well as that all-important book. If the venue is large enough and open to the public, put out some flyers well in advance, giving the exact dates and times. Provide the manager with a copy of your media kit and offer to provide a couple of printed posters for the store. (Hint: Vistaprint can produce large-size posters and even banners relatively cheaply.) Depending on the cooperative nature of the news media where you live, you can try listing your event on their local news broadcasts or in a "What's Happening" column in the local paper. And be sure you talk to the business's manager well in advance to arrange things like a refreshment table, a signing desk, a display rack, and other amenities you may want—like a microphone to use for a short book talk.

Wherever you choose, be sure to spread the word and break out the streamers and balloons. Serve up some fancy tidbits—maybe including foods from your story. Pop a few corks and turn up the music. Put your book on display and have a helper encourage guests to buy a copy of this first edition. Enjoy your fame for the day.

A Virtual Book Launch

I tried a different approach for the release of my first Civil War novel, *Beyond All Price*. Because I am a firm believer in the future of the e-book, it seemed fitting to have an e-party. It was also cheaper, of course, and a bit less self-congratulatory, to use the internet for the book's introduction, rather than just holding a small party for the folks I knew. Here's how I went about it.

My publishing imprint is Katzenhaus Books, and the company website was already up and running at Vistaprint. I wanted the launch to be connected to that site somehow, but at the same time separate and unique. The answer was a second site, accessible to me for a four-month period, but one that the general public would not see until the opening of the launch party. I started planning the party in July 2010, just as soon as I had finished approving the final manuscripts for both the paperback and the Kindle editions. The launch itself took place in September.

The party website had many pages, starting with a welcome page that set a festive tone with balloons and confetti. The book had a full page, with pictures of the cover, the cover blurb, an excerpt, and links to the company website, including the ordering information. Next came a fun page—what's a party without a few games? There were some bad jokes, a mystery puzzle, and a cartoon cat video, among other oddities. Refreshments required imagination. Visitors found a virtual buffet table with pictures of the food on offer and the recipes if they wanted to do some cooking. All the items on the buffet were dishes from the novel. Door prizes and giveaways had a separate page, which also included an opt-in box so that I could begin to create a dedicated email list.

The real key to the success of the party, however, came from my guests—seven authors and seven internet experts who wrote about writing. I interviewed the writers and provided transcripts of our discussions. The bloggers wrote articles about their specialties —everything from creating a website to the value of visiting their home towns, proofreading, punctuation, and the future of the publishing industry. Each guest had a featured page for an eight-hour period during the launch. There the guests could post their picture, pictures of their books, list their internet addresses, and invite followers. All these materials were accessible for the entire launch period and a month afterward through a list of guest links.

I cannot begin to praise my guests enough. They not only took the time to write their articles and interviews; they also publicized the launch for me on their blogs, websites, and social networks. When well-known authors sent a tweet that said, "I'll be appearing at this book launch at this time at this URL," their fans and readers came to visit and learned about my book along the way. The guest authors' and experts' help was invaluable!

Questions remain, however. Was it successful? Would I do it again? What would I change? Well, for starters, I found out the party lasted too long. I thought I was cutting back from the only other online launch party I had seen—one that ran for an entire seven-day period. Mine started on Wednesday with a respectable number of visitors. The visits peaked around noon on Thursday, and limped through Friday, falling off to near nothing by Friday evening. I should have stopped Thursday night.

The fun and games page did not attract many visitors. People who took the time to attend the party wanted to know about my book or what my guests had to say. That was a good thing, of course. They came because they were interested in the book, not for other entertainment. The opt-in box appeared in an awkward place. It should have been at the front of the site, not buried in the back. On the plus side, people loved the recipes from the book and reacted well to most of my guests. Who doesn't love food and insider information?

Sales were slow but steady through the first two days. I didn't sell as many copies as I would have liked, but those who ordered the book were new customers, most of whom I would not have met if it had not been for the launch party. And sales continued at the same steady pace for several weeks after the actual book release. I also gained new Twitter followers and Facebook friends. I'm glad I did it, although I didn't repeat the experiment for my later books.

A Virtual Book Tour

Traditional book publishers used to celebrate their new releases by sending the authors on a cross-country book tour. Sounds glamorous, doesn't it? But the practice has become prohibitively expensive—and in this age of instant communications—unnecessary. Personally, after financing one short book tour, I swore I'd never do another. Why? The author spends lots of time and money traveling from book store to library to coffee shop, never knowing whether the proprietor will have set up a successful get-together or not. Oh, I had some lovely experiences. In Charleston, South Carolina, the county library put on a lavish spread of *hors d'oeuvres* and attracted a large and attentive audience. I sold a goodly number of copies, signed every one of them, and felt like a celebrity.

But the very next day, I found myself sitting in an empty book store—one whose owner had forgotten I was coming and had done no publicity at all. It was the day before a holiday weekend in a resort town full of visitors, and there was even a local tie to the book. But for three solid hours, not one soul entered the store. The lonely clerk and I made small talk as long as we could manage, and I ended up buying books from her just to make her feel better. I also absorbed the cost of a three-hour drive and an overnight motel stay, along with meals. I felt like a failure, and the glow from the previous day's library visit faded when I looked at the negative balance in my account book.

A virtual book tour, on the other hand, is a fantastic device for building your following. Every time you visit the blog of someone new and post an interesting article, you get a chance to add that person's followers to your own. So look for bloggers with interests similar to your own, read their blogs until you are sure you like them (and their audiences), and then ask if you can do a guest post for them. If you offer their readers some information of value, you may create a long-term relationship that works for both of you.

So how do you do a virtual book tour? Here are the steps to follow. Identify a period of two or three weeks during which you can devote nearly all your time to making the virtual tour work. You won't be traveling, but you'll be writing a new blog for every stop, doing promotional ads before each visit, and responding to comments and questions from many new readers. A friend recently finished a successful month-long tour and pronounced herself thoroughly exhausted. Don't start this campaign expecting it to be easy.

Identify bloggers who welcome guest appearances and whose readers are similar to your target audience. You can't sell much historical fiction on a "Guns and Ammo" website. Look for blogs that have more readers than you do, but don't expect to find a welcome on a blog that already has thousands and thousands of followers. You're hoping to establish a long-term relationship with other writers like yourself, small-time bloggers with whom you can exchange appearances.

Contact each blogger with a personalized message that stresses what you have to offer. Here's another use for that media kit. Send your book information, a good review, a press release, and your contact information. Provide a free copy of your book. Explain the kinds of content you can offer—an interview, a blog on a particular topic, a contest in which you provide the prizes, or a book review. Be sure to check each site to see if it suggests rules for such inquiries, and don't forget to include the dates of your tour.

Promote your appearances on Twitter, Networked Blogs, an event page on Facebook, or on your Author Central page on Amazon. Your host will appreciate the advance publicity, and you'll both gain additional readers.

Provide your host with your materials, including contact information, your professional photograph, and links to your sites well in advance of the date. On the day of your appearance, check the site frequently and respond to all comments as quickly as possible. And finally, follow up with a thank you note and an offer to reciprocate.

In It for the Long Haul

The first few days or weeks of your book launch will be exhilarating, and you won't mind putting in all the extra time it takes to get the word out and promote those early sales. But you are about to learn another valuable lesson about self-publishing. It has no end! With a traditional book publisher, the practice is usually "Up or Out." For the first few weeks or months, the publisher, agent, and author will work together to sell as many books as possible, to gather dozens of believable and glowing reviews, and to break into the exalted ranks of *The New York Times* best-seller lists. Agents and publishers will pressure book stores to display new releases on a table right inside the door or on a dedicated rack or the end cap of a shelving unit. The book itself will have a short shelf-life. If your name is not a household word and the book is not on the best-seller lists within six months, it will start the long journey of shame. The store will move it to the back of the display, to the shelves of a genre rack where only the spine faces outward, and finally to the remainder table out on the sidewalk. And from there, it goes to a warehouse for the removal of its cover, a sale to a bulk paper company, or the trash pile.

Print-on-demand books and electronic editions, however, will outlive you. You can't kill them off if you try! Do you remember my story about my first success on NaNoWriMo, when I sent my manuscript off to CreateSpace to take advantage of their generous offer to print one free copy of every winning book? The product was frightful but deathless. It's still out there. When I open my CreateSpace account, one of the listings is for my *Gideon's Ladies*. They currently list it as incomplete, but I have failed in several attempts to remove it from my listing. It's sitting there waiting for me to come back and add the finishing touches, but I can't put it out of its misery.

One advantage of self-publishing, of course, is that some books, like some children, are slow to mature. Without the sales pressure of agents and big-name publishers, many such books linger for years before word-of-mouth or some other catalyst propels them into new-found popularity. What does that mean for the independent author? It means you have to keep working and marketing and promoting your books. Your list of published works may grow, but it will never get shorter. Books that sell only small numbers of copies still appear on Amazon year after year. They are beautiful examples of the hope that will not die.

Solutions to Marketing *a la* Amazon

There's an old joke about how one handles an 800-pound gorilla. The answers usually include saying "Yes, Sir!" and giving him whatever he wants. For indie writers and self-publishers, the 800-pound gorilla has always been Amazon. It dominates today's book world, selling more books than anyone else, newcomer or traditional publisher. No one seems to have exact figures because they change minute by minute, but a safe estimate is that Amazon has something in the range of ten million books available on its website. Of course, that is partially because no book ever goes out of print on their digital side.

From the time I first established my little self-publishing imprint back in 2009, I argued against allowing Amazon to gain complete control of my work. Certainly, I published my books on the Kindle site and used the Amazon-affiliated CreateSpace to print and circulate my paperback editions. But I was also determined to utilize as many other sales outlets as possible. I always recommended Smashwords for its ability to place electronic versions in the Barnes and Noble and Apple iBook catalogs, as well as on an ever-increasing number of smaller book distribution sites. It cost me more to get my books formatted for different sellers, but I thought it was worth it, and for a while, it was.

I also spoke out against Amazon's new schemes to get writers to give them exclusivity over certain books. The promises of more support, free days, new promotions, and things like paying lending libraries just didn't seem worth giving one company a monopoly over publication. However, things change quickly in the publishing world, and I have slowly begun to realize that many of these changes are reader-driven. Those who believe in a free-market system (and I do) need to listen when the market speaks.

In the past five years, the value of using multiple distribution channels has eroded noticeably. In 2010, I could count on selling some 500 books a year through Smashwords with royalties of approximately $2.00 per book—well worth paying someone $50.00 to format a new manuscript for Apple and B&N. Then—steadily—the numbers declined. In the first two months of 2016, I sold exactly three books (the total from 18 sales channels) through Smashwords, at a profit of $4.26. And meanwhile, formatting charges increased to $100.00. It was simply no longer economically possible to justify avoiding exclusivity.

What has happened? I don't have some magic explanation, but when I look at my Kindle sales, I see steady growth; when I look at Smashwords, steady decline. Apparently, the people who read my books have made a choice, for whatever may be their reasons, to do their book buying on Amazon. And if that's where my readers are, that's where I need to be as well.

Now, most of my books are available exclusively on Amazon. That makes them eligible for inclusion in the Kindle Owners' Lending Library and on the list of free books available to Prime customers. Within hours of registering with Kindle Select, someone borrowed a copy of *Damned Yankee* and read 190 pages. Readers who have purchased any of my books from other sites can rest assured that the copies are still in the archives there. So if the dog eats your Nook, you can download another copy of my books from Smashwords. However, if you want to make a new purchase, you will have to do so on Amazon.

Boxed Sets

In 2014, Amazon and the other e-book retailers began encouraging the publication of boxed sets. Two varieties were available—single or multiple authors. An author might choose to gather several older books in a series. Or a group of writers could get together and combine one book apiece on a single theme. The retailers promoted this idea as a way to bring new life into an older book or to tap into new communities of readers. One group of mystery writers tried producing an anthology of short books from a variety of authors. Because each one of them pitched to a different set of readers, writers were reaching readers who might never have heard of them otherwise.

In my case, I decided to box the first four books of my series on *The Civil War in South Carolina's Low Country*. There were production problems from the beginning. The formatting isn't too complicated, but it's tedious because you need to remove some markups in the originals and then replace them. My old brain didn't want to mess with it, so I hired someone to reformat the four books, combine them into one file and hyperlink all the chapters. My cover designer worked hard to come up with an image that included all four titles. And just when we thought we had the perfect 3-D portrait of a boxed set, Apple iBooks changed their requirements to outlaw all 3-D images, and the other retailers fell into line. Another delay followed while the designer came up with an entirely different cover.

Once again, the major selling point was that the combined set carried a price that was considerably lower than the original cost of buying all the individual volumes. But in spite of the bargain price, my readers shunned the idea. I watched the sales figures and witnessed people bypassing the boxed set to order all four of the books as separate files. I thought I was promoting the boxed set heavily, but people kept right on ordering single copies of those four books at their regular price. For example, I sold eight copies of *A Scratch with the Rebels* during the week the boxed set went live.

What went wrong? In some cases, I learned, the boxed files were too big to be downloaded unless the purchaser had access to high-speed internet services. Others found the 1300-page file confusing and too hard to navigate. A boxed set seemed like a good idea, except for the reality that nobody wanted one.

Countdowns

One of the characteristics of e-book publication in 2014 was the appearance of new marketing tricks. For example, KDP Select now offered an option to hold a "Countdown" sale. In this promotion, your book started out at a base price of $0.99 and then the price gradually increased until it reached the book's list price. Amazon continues to promote these countdowns heavily, but I fail to see the point. If customers won't buy the book for 99 cents, why would they be more likely to buy it when the price increases by one dollar, and then by two dollars?

Still, I was willing to give it a try. I listed a countdown for a book that had been out for two years and had sold regularly although in small quantities. Amazon encouraged me to help the sale along by posting frequent reminders that "there are only x-number of hours left before the price goes up." How annoying is that—not just for readers and potential customers, but also for the author who has to keep track of the hours and post the warnings?

There was not a single sale during the countdown promotion. I received no feedback on why readers did not purchase the book at a lower price, but the message was clear. Potential customers were ignoring it. The countdown did not produce any sense of urgency. They knew the book would still be around if they needed it because e-books are always available.

KDP Select and Free Days

In March and April of 2017, I experimented with Amazon's "KDP Select" program. One of the main advantages, they say, is that an author can plan several "Free Days" promotions. The concept seems clear, and it follows a well-known advertising pattern. When a new Starbucks opens, they offer free samples, hoping that one taste will bring customers back again. In the same way, offering some of one's books for free promotes more readership, and the effect carries over when the promotion is finished. Readers who sample one book are expected to be more willing to purchase other volumes by the same author.

Did it work? To a certain extent, it did, but I have a few doubts. At first, enthusiasm ran high for the books I offered for free. A few readers chose to download *The Dilemma of Arnulf of Lisieux* during the free promotion. Sales for that particular title doubled over the next six weeks, although the total for that twenty-year-old book was not exactly overwhelming.

The larger effect, however, had to do with the next promotion, where downloads of *A Scratch with the Rebels* were ten times as numerous. And after that, the promotion of *Beyond All Price* took off for the stratosphere. Downloads mounted into the hundreds, a multiple of 100 books downloaded for every one of the *Dilemma* downloads. So it works, right?

Maybe not! The enthusiasm did not last. By the time I opened the giveaway offer for *The Road to Frogmore*, readers appeared to be tired. Giveaway numbers fell off again, down to about twenty-five percent of the previous offer. But what was worse, regular sales started to fall off, too.

Now I understand that there are readers out there with good intentions but poor follow-through. They snatch up a free book, planning to read it, but somehow, it just never gets opened. I've done that myself. So the reader who has now downloaded three books but not started any of them may be disinclined to add a fourth to the good-intentions pile. OK, fair enough. You probably lose interest in a cup of coffee that has been allowed to get cold, too.

But I wonder if there isn't something else going on. I recently reviewed my own reading patterns in my Kindle library and I find that the more I pay for a book, the more inclined I am to read it, regardless of content—something about belonging to a generation that learned "you get what you pay for." (Which may be why people are still willing to pay more for a Starbucks coffee than they are for a similar beverage at McDonalds.)

One final reminder: the jury is still out on Amazon's "Kindle Owner's Lending Library" program. My books have been enrolled for several months now, and I am pleasantly surprised to see how many people have joined the paid-subscription plan that allows them to read as many books as they like. The reports that come to me show only the number of pages read, not the number of readers, but the page totals are in the thousands—higher than I expected. The benefit there, from my point of view, is that I get paid something for each page read. It amounts to approximately $0.0047 per page, but it's still an income generator.

The Value of Book Contests

Would you ever consider paying someone $100.00 for the privilege of entering a book contest? Sound like a scam? Well, think again. Book contests can help your marketing efforts in many ways. Granted, $100.00 is a lot of money to someone who is only selling a few books a month, and that amount does not cover the cost of the book itself or your mailing costs, either. But a charge of $100.00 or less is usually a legitimate one. Running a book contest is an expensive proposition. After all, someone has to pay for medals, winner's stickers, websites, postage, ads, and all the other related expenses. By charging relatively small fees, the sponsors of these contests are making it possible to reward many more fledgling authors.

Are you afraid the contest is a scam? If it has been operating for several years, you should be able to find a list of past winners. A legitimate contest should be listed in publications like *Writers Markets* or on the websites of the sponsoring organizations. By all means, do your homework, and find an award program that appears reputable and designed for writers like yourself. Then read the rules and jump in.

Are you afraid of rejection? Failure is something you might as well get used to if you've decided to become a writer. Every one of us could paper a room with our rejection letters. Lots of books just don't make it. I saw a statistic recently that indicated that out of 1.2 million books published in the past year, only about 3000 of them will ever sell more than 50,000 copies. So welcome to the 99.75% of us who should not quit our day jobs. We all flounder together. A book contest may be just what you need to overcome that fear of failure. Even if you don't win a thing, you'll benefit.

You may be surprised to find that the very act of entering a contest makes you feel more confident about your abilities. After all, you have written a book that meets the qualifications of an organization that awards good writing. You've followed guidelines and met a deadline. Best of all, you've proved to yourself that you have faith in your work. That's important.

If you don't win, be sure to follow up. Many such contests are willing to provide you with their reviewers' comments so that you can learn what it was that they did not like about your book. If you can learn from your first attempt, you'll have a better shot at future contests. Take a look at the winners. Read their books or at least excerpts from them, so that you get an idea of what the reviewers liked about them. That's another lesson learned.

And what if you do win? Even if you get nothing but an honorable mention sticker to put on your book, it will draw attention to your work and perhaps even help you sell more books. Publishers, agents, book sellers, and buyers are all impressed by those shiny little seals. A gold seal makes you stand out from that whole crowd of 1.2 million book authors. Win just one award, at any level, and you can call yourself an award-winning author. Put that on your website, display the seal or your medal everywhere you can, and use the award as a major factor in your marketing efforts.

In 2011, I entered two contests—the Pinnacle Book Achievement Awards and the annual Military Writers Society of America Book Awards. Neither one offered the equivalent of a Pulitzer or a Man Booker prize, but I profited greatly from both. Both contests give awards in many genres and are open to both traditional publishers and self-publishers. Both publish reviews of their book entries, and any self-publisher can use another book review. Remember that getting favorable publicity is a major part of your marketing effort.

Pinnacle Awards, presented by the North American Booksellers Exchange (NABE), come out every three months, but the award seal does not give dates. I won my "Best Historical Fiction" award for Summer 2011, but the seal shows only the prize, not the year. The Military Writers Society of America (MWSA) presented the same book a bronze medal for Biography. Again, the resulting seal shows only the award, not the date or genre. As soon as these contests announced their winners, my book sales began to improve. The NABE award resulted in my book being given a prominent display at two major book trade shows on the west coast. To receive my medal from MWSA, I traveled to their convention, where I met wonderfully friendly and supportive writers. I am much the richer for the experiences these contests have given me. They were well worth the entry fees.

The final word? If you don't sell your book, no one else will do it for you. But before you launch a major marketing plan, be sure you are giving your customers what they want at a price they can afford.

EPILOGUE

"What's the Bottom Line?"

"Hello! It's me again, The Second Mouse. Back when we started this new edition, you asked about money, and I told you we'd talk about that later. Well, the time has come."

"OK, all these suggestions have been helpful, but I'm still worried about what becoming a self-publisher is going to cost me. It sounds expensive."

"That depends."

"On what?"

"On your skills and abilities, your resources, and your willingness to devote a lot of time to the effort."

"Uh-oh! I don't have a whole lot of any of those. Maybe I'd be better off trying to land a traditional publishing contract."

"Better off? How so?"

"Well, I've always heard that the Big Five publishers pay their authors an advance before the book ever comes out. They pay royalties. And they handle all that technical stuff, like designing a cover, doing the layouts and conversions, and getting publicity for the book."

"Let's start with the advance payment. You do understand, don't you, that the full term is 'an advance against royalties?' That means that eventually, your book must earn enough in royalties to pay the publisher back. Let's say you receive an early payment of $5000.00. The publisher will send your check to your agent, who will smoothly extract her fifteen-percent commission and then issue you a check for just $4250.00.

"Now let's assume that your publishing contract says you will receive a five percent royalty on every book sale. If your book retails for $20.00, you'll get $1.00 of that amount. The other $19.00 goes to the publisher, all the people they employ to do that technical stuff, the distributor, and the retailer. But before you start receiving royalty checks, you have to sell enough books to pay back the entire advance—all $5000.00 of it. Only after the first 5000 copies have sold will you start seeing any royalties, and even then, you'll only be getting $0.85 a copy. That's what's left after the ongoing agent's share."

"What happens if I never sell that many copies?"

"That will depend on your contract—which, by the way, is why you'll need to hire a lawyer to look over that contract before you sign it. If you fulfill all the terms of your contract, including meeting all the deadlines, making all requested changes, and showing up for any public appearances they schedule for you, then you may not owe the publisher anything. That's the risk the publisher assumes. But beware! If you fail to fulfill the signed contract, the advance will become due in full."

"So it's not such a good deal after all. But that brings me back to the original question. What does it cost to self-publish a book?"

"It's all up to you, so there's no one answer I can give you. I can show you the No-Cost Option, the Budget Package, or the Spare-No-Luxury Tour. What is your choice?"

"Well, of course, the no-cost option is the most appealing."

"Maybe. It's possible to publish a book these days without paying for anything beyond the basics you need to write a grocery list—ball-point pens and yellow legal pads or a simple computer with enough memory to hold 100,000 words or so. Once you've written your book, Kindle will let you add your .mobi file to their Kindle Store on the Amazon website at no charge. They'll sell your e-book for you, take their expenses out of the income of your sales, and send you the remainder—something like seventy percent of your list price. So if you advertise your e-book for $2.99, you'll get $2.10.

"The same general deal works on Smashwords and Create-Space. Smashwords will take your .epub file and distribute it to other online bookstores like iBooks and Kobo. Because their multiple distribution channels cost more than the Kindle store, you'll receive about sixty percent or $2.01 per book.

"CreateSpace will print and distribute the paperback versions of your book to Amazon and other brick and mortar bookstores. They will also sell copies directly through their online book store. Obviously, their charges for paper, ink, and bindings are higher than the cost of an e-book. You'll set the print price to take that into account. You might reasonably charge $18.95 for the paper edition. If that book sells on Amazon, you'll earn $6.32 or thirty-three percent. But if it goes out to one of CreateSpace's other channels, like Barnes & Noble or an independent bookstore, you'll be lucky to clear $2.53 or thirteen percent. Those royalty payments will cover your basic expenses if you do all the work yourself, but be warned. Doing all the work yourself can be time-consuming and frustrating. It's easy for me to say you can load your .epub file to Smashwords for free, but the instruction book for preparing that .epub file is thirty-six pages long, and you must follow every single point to the letter, or your upload will fail."

"That option is still financially appealing. Are there any other downsides to the do-it-yourself process?"

"Oh, yes. I've mentioned that I do a lot of judging for a major book awards contest, so I've seen more than a few horrible examples of the do-it-yourself variety. Books come through our pipeline with horrendous grammatical or mechanical errors—spelling mistakes, tiny margins, fonts that are difficult to read, unexplained gaps in the text, ugly covers on which you can't find the author's name, and other atrocities that tell us the writer is an amateur. Books with problems like that don't win awards. And they don't sell, either."

"Just for fun, tell me what the Spare-No-Expense option would cost. I assume that's where you hire professional help to do all this checking and designing and uploading for you."

"Well, it starts with purchasing all the newest word-processing packages. My recommended trio of Word, Scapple, and Scrivener will run you close to $300. Then you'll need to add in an ISBN and a Library of Congress Cataloguing number, which could cost you as much as $200.00.

"During the writing process, you may find that you need a developmental editor to help with plot, characterization, and story arc. They cost at least $50 per hour, and they work at a rate of two to five pages per hour. Then, once you've finished your manuscript, you'll also need a copy editor to catch all those horrible mistakes that creep into the best writing. Copy editors may charge by the hour or by the word. Total editing costs for a 100,000 word or 400-page manuscript will run between $2000 and $3000.

"A free-lance cover designer will charge at least $300 and could go much higher if you want specialized photography. If you let CreateSpace design your cover, it will fall between $400 and $600.

"And finally there are all the formatting costs. Smashwords (those folks with the complicated instructions) provides a list of approved formatters who will do the nasty job for about $150. CreateSpace will format your Kindle file for $139 and your print interior for $349.

"Your all-expense-paid total? Somewhere over $4500, and that's before you even start to think about promotional materials like bookmarks and business cards or traveling to do book signings and book lectures. I've gone that route, but I'll be the first to tell you that you will need a combination of hard work and phenomenal luck to sell enough copies to recoup your expenditures."

"But you said it is possible to make money as a self-publisher."

"And so it is. As a general rule, self-publishers make more money than traditionally-published authors, except for those few power-house writers like John Grisham or J. K. Rowling."

"How?"

"By learning the trade—learning it well—and doing it themselves."

"What's your approach?"

"I've gradually been increasing my knowledge and skills. And each time I gain the ability to complete a task on my own, I cut down on my expenses. At the moment, I'm on the Budget Package. I still hire a cover designer because I have no artistic talents. She charges around $300.00. I've purchased another set of ten ISBNs which cost me $30 apiece instead of the $125 for an individual number. I've also discovered an online application for my Library of Congress number, so I no longer have to pay CreateSpace $75.00 to handle that for me. Now the LOCC will only cost me the postage it will take to send one copy of the book to Washington, DC.

"In the past year, I've updated all my word processing and planning software and added two entirely new programs to handle editing and layout design. Those purchases have amounted to about $600. However, I know I'll use the same software for at least the three books I currently have in the pipeline so that I can amortize the cost per book to around $200. My total for the last book I created was about $565.00. Once I sell my first two hundred copies—some digital and some print versions—I should be starting to see a profit."

"Three books at once?"

"Sure. One's a novel almost ready to hit the shelves after some last-minute tweaking. Then there's this one I'm still working on, and the third idea for a novel is bouncing around in my brain, waiting for me to start outlining it. That's part of the secret to making money with self-publishing. You have to keep writing."

"So what has been your overall result? Have you made money or are you studying to become a fry cook?"

"I see you remember my original plan. I was going to produce my first independent book within two years. I needed to sell enough copies to (1) restore the savings account and (2) accumulate enough of a cushion to finance any future book. I gave myself an estimated eighteen months to two years to accomplish that. If at the end of four years, I had not made a profit, I would retire from the publishing business and take up knitting or crossword puzzles—or flipping burgers.

"I was incredibly lucky. *Beyond All Price* languished unnoticed for over a year. Then, thanks to a free deal on Amazon, its sales figures took off. Within the next four months, I made more than enough to return every dollar I had borrowed. The rest went into the business account to pay for future publications. Since then, the account has fluctuated but has never fallen into another deficit. I haven't had another best-seller, but sales have been good enough to replenish the publishing costs slowly.

"I have published eleven books of various types, and I expect my profits to increase slowly but steadily. In the beginning, you asked about paying the bills. I still can't rely on my writing to pay the mortgage. But it does pay for itself with small amounts left over so that I can continue to claim that writing is my business, not my hobby. I see that as a victory. I wish you the same success."

www.ingramcontent.com/pod-product-compliance
Lightning Source LLC
Chambersburg PA
CBHW071657090426
42738CB00009B/1558